Thou
  Shalt
    Remember

Thou
Shalt
Remember

Lessons of a Lifetime

HANNAH HURNARD

1817

Harper & Row, Publishers, San Francisco

Cambridge, Hagerstown, New York, Philadelphia, Washington
London, Mexico City, São Paulo, Singapore, Sydney

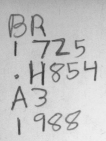
Some of the incidents in this book have been told in somewhat different form in the author's earlier published works.

THOU SHALT REMEMBER: LESSONS OF A LIFETIME. Copyright © 1988 by Hannah Hurnard. All rights reserved. Printed in the United States of America. No part of this book may be used or reproduced in any manner whatsoever without written permission except in the case of brief quotations embodied in critical articles and reviews. For information address Harper & Row, Publishers, Inc., 10 East 53rd Street, New York, N.Y. 10022. Published simultaneously in Canada by Fitzhenry & Whiteside, Limited, Toronto.

Library of Congress Cataloging-in-Publication-Data

Hurnard, Hannah.
    Thou shalt remember.

    1. Hurnard, Hannah.   2. Christian biography.
3. Converts from Judaism—Biography.   4. Missionaries—
Israel—Biography.   I. Title.
BR1725.H854A3 1988   209'.2'4   [B]   87–46212
ISBN 0–06–064094–4 (pbk.)

88   89   90   91   92   FG   10   9   8   7   6   5   4   3   2   1

Contents

1	Thou Shalt Remember	1
2	The Land of Bondage and Affliction	5
3	The Passover from Bondage into Liberty	12
4	Manna in the Wilderness	20
5	The Pillar of Cloud and Pillar of Fire	27
6	Crossing the Red Sea	32
7	The Bitter Waters at Marah	41
8	The Twelve Springs at Elim	49
9	Seventy Palm Trees	56
10	Food from Heaven in the Desert of Sihn	62
11	Massah	69
12	The Amalekites	74
13	Jehovah Nissi, the Lord Our Banner	82
14	Jethro, the Priest of Midian	90
15	The Workers Who Helped Moses	100
16	The Mountain Smoked	109
17	The Thick Darkness Where God Was	114
18	On the Mount with God	119
19	The Glory of the Lord on the Mountaintop	124
20	Building a Sanctuary for the Lord to Dwell In	130
21	A Mercy Seat of Pure Gold	136
22	The Cherubim on the Mercy Seat	143
23	Show Me Thy Glory	150
24	A Merciful and Gracious God	155
25	The Lord Will Do Marvels	160
26	The Presence of God	165
27	Holiness in the Lord	171
28	The Glory of the Lord Filled the Tabernacle	178
	The Lessons Learned in My Lifetime	182

1

Thou Shalt Remember

"Thou shalt remember all the way that the Lord thy God led thee forty years in the wilderness:
To humble thee. to prove thee; to know what was in thine heart, whether thou wouldest keep his commandments or no."

DEUTERONOMY 8:2 KJV

WHAT A WONDERFUL THING it is to possess a memory, with power to recall all the experiences and lessons we have learned in the School of Earth Experience!

I have just reached my eightieth birthday and have been inspired by the loving Lord to peruse the pages in my Book of Memory with awed thankfulness and joy. With him I have been looking at the record and the images of a long lifetime of experiences and blessings. I have recalled ever so many mighty acts of the Lord God and his loving power revealed in the experiences through which I have passed.

It has been possible by the aid of memory to decipher the causes of many astonishing events and to realize that nothing has ever taken place by chance; everything has been the result of what I have said and done and the ways in which I have expressed my thoughts, desires, emotions, and reactions to every circumstance in which I found myself. Looking back has solved what seemed at the time to be many confusing aspects of my life.

How many bewildering questions we human beings find ourselves asking during our daily lives here on earth! We ask:

1. By whom or by what power was I sent here?
2. Where did I come from?
3. Where am I going?
4. Why do I find myself on earth in the body of a human being and not that of an animal or bird or fish?
5. Why was I born in the home and family of two particular people?
6. Why did I find myself born into certain circumstances and not utterly different ones?
7. What was I sent here to do?
8. What are the purpose and plan that I am to fulfill?
9. Why was I born into a fallen world with all its sorrows and sufferings and where such seemingly crazy behavior is so often manifested?
10. Why are all the circumstances and situations in which I find myself continually changing?
11. Why am I being inexorably led along a path of mortal life toward the gateway of death, where I shall make my exit from this realm of consciousness into a completely different one?
12. Or will it be into no consciousness at all?
13. Am I now after all these years of experience the same person that I was when I entered into mortal life through the gate of birth?
14. Do I manifest the same nature and qualities of character that I manifested many years ago or completely different ones?
15. Why have I continually been filled with strange, powerful, nostalgic longings for something completely unlike all earthly things, as though I have left something behind and lost all idea of what it was but have been passionately longing to rediscover and possess it once again?
16. What do I truly long for?

This special perusal of the Book of Memory since my eightieth birthday has reminded me in a wonderful way of these and many more questions and also of fascinating answers that have shone into my mind and understanding as the years have passed by.

When I was still a small child my father gave me a diary and encouraged me to write something in it every day, and this habit has continued throughout my lifetime. One of the first entries in that first diary is written in big, scrawly letters: "Today we had chicken for dinner and missionary for supper!" I sometimes find myself wondering whether the things we inscribe in our Books of Memory often look, in God's sight, as infantile as that long ago entry looks to me now.

What has been the happy result of *remembering all the way the Lord God has led me* and looked after me so lovingly and tenderly for sixty-one years since I became conscious of his Presence with me as a girl of nineteen? What glorious vistas of radiant truth and spiritual illumination has he given to me?

In a beautiful and challenging way they are summed up in the words in Deuteronomy 8:2, written at the beginning of this chapter:

All the way in which the Lord thy God led thee, ... To humble thee, and to prove thee, to know what was in thine heart; whether thou wouldest keep his commandments or no.

Surely these are the purposes for experiencing earthly life:

1. That we may be helped to learn childlike humility; that we may be willing to be taught spiritual laws that are vitally important and that we could not possibly discover for ourselves, as they can be revealed only to those who *come to know him*, our true Father God.

2. To discover everything hidden away in our own hearts— the nature of our ruling desires, attitudes, and emotional reactions to everything that happens to us.

3.   To be tested and examined to see whether we can prove that we love the Lord God and long to obey his commandments or not; and if we have been continually practicing the lessons we have been learning here in the School of Earth Experience.

The following chapters in this book contain the results of looking back in the light of the tender, loving, and holy presence of the Lord God and learning from him whether or not his divine purpose in sending me here to school on earth has been fulfilled or still awaits fuller development. Have I learned to realize that all the words and actions I have expressed have been creative and that they form my nature and character in the sight of my Father Creator God?

It is with joy and awed gratitude that I seek to share in this book the main lessons he has lovingly taught me during the years of my life. Perhaps in this way I may be privileged to share some of the radiant joy and holy thanksgiving of my heart with those who read this book.

2

The Land of Bondage and Affliction

*And the Lord said, I have surely seen the affliction of my people
... and have heard their cry by reason of their taskmasters; for I
know their sorrows; and I am come down to deliver them.*

EXODUS 3:7, 8 KJV.

THE FOUNDATIONAL TRUTH I learned in the School of Earth
Experience is this: we are spiritual beings who can never find
true satisfaction and happiness except by recovering our lost
God-consciousness and uniting our wills with his.

The first nineteen years of my life can be symbolized by the
period during which the Children of Israel suffered bondage in
Egypt at the hands of Pharaoh's cruel taskmasters.

I was born into what, from a worldly point of view, looked like
privileged circumstances. My parents were devoted and earnest
lovers of God and longed to live every day doing his will with
joyful eagerness. They were entrusted by him with abundant financial means, which they faithfully shared with others who were
in special need. At the same time they sought to lead those persons to true faith in God.

Surely it was a wonderful blessing to be the child of such
parents, born into such easy and prosperous conditions. But in
fact, from earliest childhood, it seemed to me to be exactly opposite, for I had what I found to be especially painful handicaps.

I suffered ceaselessly from terrifying fears, most of them imaginary but made vividly real to me by the physical feelings that accompanied them, turning my life into a nightmare. Uncontrollable fear of darkness made the approach of each evening a time of increasing dread and fright. When I lay in bed, the fear became so painful that I screamed again and again and even began walking in my sleep, desperately trying to find some light.

Worse than that was a continual fear of dying and of being put in a box and then buried in the ground forever, unable to escape though always conscious. This caused intense claustrophobic terror of being shut in anywhere. I never dared to lock a door or even close one properly, in case I would not be able to open it again. Of course, later when I went to school and whenever visitors were staying in the house, as was nearly always the case, this inabililty to bring myself to lock even the bathroom door became embarrassing and overwhelmingly humiliating.

The claustrophobic dread and constant fears that afflicted me may well have been due to the fact that my mother experienced excruciating and long, drawn-out pain, far beyond anything normal, while she was giving birth to me at home. It seemed to her, and probably to me, the baby, that I would never be able to escape into freedom and life, and when at last the birth did take place, I appeared to be dead. It soon became apparent that I would never be a natural and happy child.

Another difficulty was that from the time I began to try to speak, I developed a distressing stutter and was often unable to do anything but grimace, make ugly sounds, and dribble and even spit. I brought a proud nature into this earth life and found this particular handicap overwhelmingly humiliating. This was especially the case when I entered school, where I could never speak properly nor answer any of the questions asked in class and so appeared to be a complete dunce. This awakened in me an intense dislike of human beings and of having to make contact with others, which in certain cases grew into real hatred.

Only one person seemed able to soothe my pangs of fear and give me some kind of comfort, and that was my father. I clung to him with passionate, despairing longing that I never be anywhere where he was not. But both he and my mother were busy people and had to be away from the house a great deal of each day, and the desperate realization that I could not run to him for relief and comfort grew ever greater. Not unnaturally, it seemed to others that I was continually trying to draw attention to myself and also to get my father to give me everything that I desired, and that my behavior was not to be encouraged.

I felt as though I was imprisoned in a world of tormenting terrors and bodily distress from which it seemed there was no escape. I emphasize these facts at some length because multitudes of other children suffer in the same or still worse ways, and many parents or caregivers either do not know how to help them or actually make the situation far worse. I long to share in this book the reassuring fact that there is a wonderful key that can open the door of this terrible prison of fear and lead to perfect deliverance and liberty.

I remember clearly as a little child of four years old, standing evening after evening during the summer under one of the great trees in the beautiful garden that surrounded our home. Looking up at the sunset sky I would sob heartbrokenly, "Is there anybody anywhere in the world as lonely and frightened as I am? O God! People say that you are there and are loving and kind, and I have only to ask you to help me and you will do so, but you never do. Aren't you really there after all? Is there no one anywhere who can make me feel safe and not afraid?"

Just three times during those first years I experienced temporary relief and release into a different realm of beauty and even pleasure, though never happiness. When I was four years old and then six and eight years, I was taken by my parents with a group of relatives and friends to spend some winter weeks in the beauties of Switzerland. There the mountains with their shining white peaks turning a glorious rosy pink and red at sunset and sunrise exercised an enchanting effect upon me. The beauty of the snow and pine woods and the shining cloudless blue skies seemed to arouse in me the certainty that once, somewhere, I had known and experienced a condition of being in a realm of overwhelming beauty, safety, and happy companionship with loving beings to whom I could speak without stuttering. In that place there was no night nor any kind of darkness and no gaping holes in the earth into which bodies were put and covered over and left forever. How my heart ached with longing to find my way back into that vanished world of peace and joy! Those Swiss mountains haunted me ever after and kept alive in me a bittersweet yearning to return to my true lost home and family once again.

After the third visit to Switzerland, the First World War broke out. I was nine years old. Constant air raid sirens, complete blackouts night after night without a glimmer of light anywhere, and all the changes involved in daily life completely shattered my nerves and brought things to a crisis. Again and again at school and also in the streets I would fall headlong to the ground and lie there shrieking and shaking with terror, to the great embarrassment or disgust of my schoolmates and others.

Then the doctor told my parents that I must be taken away from school for a time (several years it proved to be) and be taught at home. Oh, the unutterable relief of it! A kind young woman was found who came to live with us and to teach me. She also helped my mother, who was left with a huge rambling house to look after, as one after another the staff of servants was called up to do war work.

Though things did become easier for some years, it seemed as though my nerves would never recover and that for the rest of my life I would be friendless and isolated from others and unable to live a normal life. In fact, at times I was so desperate that I was often tempted to commit suicide, but, thank God, I was afraid to do so. So until I was nineteen years old I never knew what it was like to feel happy.

My parents were always wonderfully kind and yearned almost heartbrokenly to help me in every possible way. The sorrow and anxiety that I caused them, especially during my night terrors, was evident to everyone except myself. So the years symbolic of the bondage and terrible sufferings of the Children of Israel in the land of Egypt dragged slowly by, seeming to a child like an endless eternity. After they ended and a stupendous deliverance arrived, for a long time I could hardly bear to look back on that period of loneliness, affliction, and despair. I used to wonder how the loving God who had at last made himself real to me and rescued me in such a wondrous way could possibly bear to allow helpless little children to suffer as I had done, and for so long. Also I wondered why he had allowed my parents to suffer such grief and distress.

But looking back at those long ago pages in my Book of Memory, I came to understand why it was all permitted. Now my heart overflows with adoring gratitude that I was allowed to come to earth to experience those conditions, and I am especially thankful that they were allowed to happen at the very beginning of my life, so that from the age of nineteen I could begin learning the glorious lessons that I was sent here to learn.

It was during the childhood and girlhood periods of life that I came to understand the first great truth that every fallen human being must discover sooner or later: we are all spiritual beings who can never find satisfaction until we are restored again to our

lost God-consciousness. Until that point we are brought into experiences that compel us to realize that without living in contact
with God, our heavenly Father, we exist in a realm of utter desolation and despair. Nothing this earthly life can offer us can
ever satisfy the true longings in our hearts but only lead us
deeper and deeper into despair and a hell of misery. Only the
Lord Jesus can show us the way to rediscover that priceless radiant life of God-consciousness, which alone can give us true
satisfaction, happiness, and peace.

So after the despair and desolation of those first nineteen years
of not being able to realize God's presence and love, for sixty-
one years, by his grace, nothing has been able to tempt me to
turn back from following him, even though the path of earthly
life has led again and again to experiences from which I would
naturally have fled in terror. But the mere thought of turning
away and breaking contact with his holy, loving will, and so finding myself once again experiencing loss of God-consciousness,
has been a great protection. It has also led continually into in-
creasingly radiant blessings such as I could never have imagined.

Now I realize why Moses kept exhorting the Children of Israel
never to forget their years of tormenting slavery in Egypt. For
with the book recording those memories continually open before them, through the long wilderness journey leading to the
Promised Land of eternal, unbroken communion with God, nothing would ever be able to tempt them to turn aside or settle
down outside their true homeland.

But a second treasure of knowledge I also owe to those years
of bondage to fear. I have become able to understand and have
compassion toward those around me who are struggling with
unendurable stresses of some kind or are in the affliction of a
nervous breakdown, whether they be children or adults. I am
also able to sympathize tenderly with those who have to be in
contact with them day and night, especially mothers with ner-

vous children who find their own nerves breaking down under the endless strain, and who perhaps compulsively and uncontrollably use physical violence to prevent the children's screams from being heard. How many battered babies there are, and also how many nervously battered and tortured mothers, relatives, or caregivers who need our compassion just as much as their helpless victims do! Those who do the cruel things need more love, not less. This is the revelation that the Lord Jesus brought to this world of fallen men and women.

With adoring wonder, as I look back over the years, I clearly see that it was those early experiences of living in bondage to fear and then finding my prison door thrown open and the way into freedom revealed that allowed me the privilege of writing a book entitled *Hinds' Feet on High Places.** It has brought comfort, reassurance, and even deliverance from slavery to fear to a great many people around the world. Surely it cannot be anything but gloriously worthwhile to have suffered for a time and then been enabled to experience the way of deliverance and to share the knowledge thus gained with others! Glory be to God indeed; he doeth all things well!

Father in Heaven, we worship and adore you. May we live continually praising and thanking you for bringing us out of the house of bondage into a good land wherein there is no scarcity nor lack of anything (Deut. 8:9, 10).

---

*Hind's Feet on High Places published by Tyndale House Publishers, Wheaton, IL, 1979.

3

The Passover from Bondage into Liberty

This is a day to remember forever—the day of leaving Egypt and your slavery, for the Lord hath brought you out with mighty miracles.

EXODUS 13:3

THE THIRD GREAT LESSON learned in the School of Earth Experience was this: *Faith* is the key to recovering our lost God-consciousness and the ability to make real contact with him. But faith is not what I had always supposed it to be. It is not believing things about God, not even that he is able to rescue and save us from enslavement to evil things. In the Bible, faith is shown to be *willingness to be obedient and to do God's will*. And unbelief is insisting upon our own will and rejecting what God shows is his will.

In the summer of 1924, when I was nineteen years of age, my father arranged for me to go with him to attend the annual Keswick Convention, a summer conference for evangelical Christians from all over the British Isles in the beautiful, mountainous county of Cumberland.

I was unwilling to go with him; indeed at first I refused to do so. I had developed an extreme dislike of all religious services at which I was supposed to worship a God who had allowed me to experience a completely desolate life for so many years and had done absolutely nothing to help me, although I had so often prayed desperately that he make himself real to me.

More and more often during my teen years I had begun to doubt whether a being called God really existed, and I had become convinced that he did not. He was just an idea invented by human beings, and it was not only a waste of time to attend services, but also completely boring. Worse still, my claustrophobic feelings made the very thought of spending hours each day in a crowded tent, surrounded by a thousand or more people, a real nightmare.

However, my father lovingly assured me that we would always sit at the end of a row on the very outskirts of the tent, so that I could get up and leave anytime I felt I must do so. Moreover, we would not stay in a crowded guest house or hotel but take lodgings just outside Keswick and use bicycles to get to the meetings. The kind young woman who had taught me during the war years and had lived with us ever since would go with us and arrange for our meals.

In the end I made a bargain with my father. I would go to one meeting in the morning and one at night, and then we must stay on for a whole week after the convention was over and enjoy the beauty and peace of the mountains alone. And so we went.

I knew how earnestly my parents were praying that the loving heavenly Father would use the speakers at the meetings to help me find deliverance from my fears and claustrophobia and the humiliating handicap of stammering. I told myself, therefore, that if God existed and was willing to reveal himself to me, it would surely be at the Keswick Convention, where a great crowd of people was gathered seeking his presence and longing to worship and serve him. Surely he would demonstrate his love and power in some obvious and visible way. Desperately I longed that he would do so.

But, alas, I went through the whole week until the last day and found no help of any kind at the meetings. God remained utterly unreal and apparently nonexistent. Between the meetings, however, as I wandered alone on the lovely hillsides or down beside beautiful Lake Derwentwater, I did find ease of mind to an unusual degree. I did not find happiness—I had no idea what that was—but physical and mental relaxation and pleasure in the majestic distant mountains and the sound of running water and the rolling fields and green trees.

The final morning of the convention dawned and I entered the great tent, as I thought for the last time. There was not one special speaker that morning but a group of missionaries from all over the world, standing up one by one and telling us of their experiences of God's love and power amid the sorrows of the heathen lands and the poverty-stricken people among whom they worked. As I listened to them and saw the joy and light that seemed to stream from their faces as they spoke of their Lord and Savior, an overwhelmingly passionate longing to find the same God filled my heart and mind. Surely he must exist after all, or they would not be able to radiate his love and joy as they described to us the miracles of his grace that they had witnessed.

I sat there shaking with longing and anguished despair. It seemed that I was the only person in the world he did not love or want to help!

The meeting lasted for three hours. When the missionaries had finished speaking, the chairman rose to his feet and asked that if any young people there had felt challenged to yield their lives to God and had heard him calling them to missionary work, would they please stand up.

I knew that while I was still in my mother's womb she and my father had dedicated me to be a missionary. They had told me so, and I had almost hated them for so doing! With my stammering mouth, terror of human beings, and a fearful nature, I longed only to be able to stay sheltered all my life in a safe home surrounded by love and kindness and tender care. How could the idea of wanting anyone, least of all me, to spend life as a missionary amid the dangers, discomforts, and persecutions in distant lands have originated? It was the most frightful of all prospects that I could imagine!

When the chairman finished speaking, hundreds of young men and women rose to their feet in response to his challenge. But I crouched glued to the bench, shrouded in a tumult of terror, anger, and desolation.

Then the chairman asked if there were any parents present who would gladly encourage their young people to become missionaries in other lands. A great number of men and women rose to their feet, and my father also stood up.

That was too much! I got up, rushed from the tent, made my way back to the cottage, and locked myself in my bedroom. There I sank on my knees beside the bed and cried aloud in utter despair, "O God, if you are there you must make yourself real to me. If you don't, I shall know that you don't exist and that there is no hope anywhere in the universe, nothing but fear and loneliness and death and the utterly terrible unknown beyond that!"

Then I siezed the little Bible that my father had given me and exclaimed, "I'm going to flap this Bible open. Christians say that it is your Word and that you speak to us through it. Speak to me now through what is written on the page at which it opens." Then I opened the Bible and looked, and it was a page in the first book of the Kings of Israel.

Horror and derision filled my heart. "There you are! That's the sort of God you are. As if anything in this book of Kings with all their names and evil doings could possibly reveal a God of love. I'm going to shut this Bible and never open it again."

Then suddenly a thought came into my mind. "Perhaps I had better give this apparently nonexistent God a chance and look at what is written on this page." And I looked and found that it was

1 Kings 18, all about the prophet Elijah up on Mount Carmel challenging the false prophets of Baal to call down fire from heaven to prove that their god really existed and could do what they asked him to do. And I read how they called upon Baal hour after hour, and "there was neither voice, nor any to answer, nor any that regarded" (v. 29 KJV).

How exactly that described my own case for so many years! No voice had answered my despairing cries for help; no sign appeared that anyone heard.

Then I read how Elijah repaired the altar of the Lord that had been broken down and laid on the altar "a sacrifice" (v. 30) and said, "Let it be known this day that thou art God."

Shuddering and trembling all over I gasped out, "Yes—that's the sort of God you are. Before you will help and make yourself real to me you insist that I offer you a sacrifice. I know what sacrifice you are going to demand from me. It is that I am to give you my stammering mouth and live trying to tell people about you by just making grimaces at them and spitting and not being able to say a word. Also you will insist that I am to become a missionary just as my parents promised I would be. Well, I won't do it. *I won't offer you that sacrifice.* It would seem to me to be an existence in hell!"

Then suddenly a devastating thought flashed into my mind. *But I'm in hell already and I don't know how to get out!*

I knelt there in agony, and then, at last, impossible as it seemed, I heard myself saying, "But if you will make yourself real to me and help me, I *will* give you my stammering mouth, and I *will* become a missionary."

Then I looked again at the open Bible on the bed before me and read, "Then the fire of the Lord fell, and consumed the burnt sacrifice. ... And all the people ... fell on their faces: and they said, The Lord, he is the God; the Lord, he is the God" (vv. 38– 39 KJV).

At that moment it was as though an iron-bound door in my heart and mind was suddenly unlocked and flung open, and *light*—warm, glorious, and radiant—engulfed me as in a sea of love. Two loving arms went around me and a tender voice said gently, "Here I am, Hannah. I have been here all the time, but you locked yourself away from consciousness of me and my presence by refusing to yield yourself and all your sorrows to me completely. Now the block has gone and you know that I am here. I love you and I will never leave you. You will never be alone again."

O my Lord! As I live again that moment as it is inscribed in my Book of Memories, it's true! For sixty-one years you have never left me alone for a single moment. How I love and adore you! I can never stop praising and thanking you forever!

Back there in that little room near Keswick I sobbed again. "O God, if you love me and are real as you seem to be now in such a wonderful way, please speak to me again and confirm this experience so that I will never doubt it nor think that it has been my imagination, because it seems as though this wondrous experience can't possibly last but will fade away like a dream. Please speak to me again as I open the Bible at some other page and read what is written there."

So I opened the Bible again and looked and read, and the very first words I saw were, "He said unto me, My grace is sufficient for thee: for my strength is made perfect in weakness" (2 Cor. 12:9 kjv).

My parents had told me that my name, Hannah, means God's grace! And it seemed as though I heard the same tender voice saying in my thoughts, "Hannah, every time you hear somebody calling you by your name, remind yourself of these words and claim them. God says that his grace is sufficient for you and his strength will be made perfect in your weakness and infirmity. And then add the rest of verse 9 and say, 'Most gladly therefore will I rather glory in my infirmities, that the power of Christ may rest upon me,' and you will be made strong to overcome everything triumphantly."

So in that little bedroom on the Cumberland hillside, the miracle happened. The years of bondage and slavery to fear and loneliness ended. In one-half hour the block was removed, and the cleansing, life-bringing fire of God's love and grace fell and consumed the sacrifice, burning up the bonds that had bound me. Nothing was altered outwardly. I still stammered and dreaded meeting other people. But everything in my thoughts and desires had been transformed. I rose from my knees a new being and went to tell my father the wonderful news.

So that was how I was taught the most glorious lesson in my life. I received back my lost treasure of knowing how to make contact with God and to unite with his divine will and so begin living in the one true realm of eternal life and spiritual consciousness of God.

I was shown the true meaning of faith, which I had never before understood. Faith is not believing things about God and religious creeds and teachings, nor is it believing that he exists and can do everything. But faith is *willingness* to do what he shows us is his will and to lay our own will and heart's desires down into death, by offering them to him as a living sacrifice upon an altar of complete surrender to him. On the other hand, unbelief is just the opposite, namely *unwillingness* to accept part or all of God's will and insisting upon going our own way and doing and getting what we want. Only God's enabling grace can make this initial surrender of self-will possible and then enable us to continue doing it day by day.

The building of the first altar of true surrender and laying down of the one chief block that prevents acceptance of God's will takes place in a great many ways in different individuals and at different ages in life. But sometime this vital surrender of self and self-consciousness must be made, so that our lost God-consciousness can again be recovered. And in order to maintain that recovered contact with God, new altars of surrender will have to be built day by day and new sacrifices of self's will be made. At first those surrenders are likely to prove difficult and costly, but we need never dread them. For we shall soon make the wondrous discovery that everything willingly laid down into death in response to God's will will be raised again in some more glorious form. And we shall know that the real meaning of sacrifice is not terrible but lovely beyond words to express. For sacrifice soon turns out to be the ecstatic experience of giving the best we have to the one we love the most and receiving the very best that he loves to give us, and in which he finds his greatest eternal joy and delight.

So the initial building of an altar of obedience to God's will continues day by day in willingness to accept and bear some deeply distressing, perhaps agonizing situation or condition. It may be in the home or at work, in one's own physical body or in the circumstances of those we love best, or it may be unfaithfulness in a married partner or persecution or threatening dangers. It is these daily and hourly altars of surrender to God's will that keep us in blissful contact with him and with his triumphant enabling power.

I look back over the pages in my Book of Memory and relive what seemed to be completely impossible challenges with the fears that sought to hold me back from making the surrender. But I recall that he never once allowed me to do so, impossible as it seemed, and that I was led, year after year, to ever greater adventures, tests, and glorious new discoveries. He has never, even in the face of the greatest dangers in terrorist-infested parts of the world, left me bereft of the sense of his presence. And more and more as the years have passed the wondrous fact has been confirmed—that sacrifice is indeed the ecstasy of giving the best we have to the one we love the most, the Divine Lover, and receiving from him his very best, too.

4

Manna in the Wilderness

Thou shalt remember ... the Lord thy God ... suffered thee to hunger, and fed thee with manna ... that he might make thee know that man doth not live by bread only, but by every word that proceedeth out of the mouth of the Lord.

DEUTERONOMY 8:2, 3 KJV

Then said the Lord ... Behold, I will rain bread from heaven for you ... Go out and gather a certain rate every day. ... And when the dew that lay was gone up, behold, upon the face of the wilderness, there lay a small round thing, as small as the hoar frost on the ground. And when the children of Israel saw it they said one to another, It is manna. ... And Moses said unto them, This is the bread which the Lord hath given you to eat.... And they gathered it every morning, every man according to his eating: and when the sun waxed hot, it melted.

EXODUS 16:4–21 KJV

THE THIRD God-given lesson was this: maintaining God-consciousness and nourishing the soul with spiritual food requires setting aside a Quiet Time for communion with God every day, preferably in the early morning.

I learned this lesson the evening of the last day of the Keswick Convention. For I attended a special meeting for young people, designed to help those who had responded to the call given at the missionary meeting in the morning.

Clarence Foster was the speaker at this farewell meeting, and God used him in a wonderful way. It was the first religious meet-

ing that I ever attended with no shrinking and dread. Instead I
went hungering and thirsting to learn all I could to help me
retain the blessed experience of the morning and not, horror of
horrors, find myself slipping back into the dark prison from
which I had so wonderfully escaped.

Clarence Foster told us that now that we had yielded our lives
to God and had offered our youth and time and strength all
through life to be used by him in any way that he showed us was
his will, it was essential that we should know how to maintain
vital daily contact with him in order to receive his enabling grace
and power and understanding of his will.

This was the one secret that I needed to learn above all others.
It seemed as though it must be more important than anything
else in the world. I drank in everything that he said like a person
who had been lost in a parched desert land and was now receiving a draught of life-giving water.

Clarence told us that the precious secret was this: we were to
meet with the Lord morning by morning as soon as we awoke
and before speaking to or making contact with anyone else. At
least half an hour or three-quarters of one should be set aside
for this purpose. During that time we should offer our minds
and hearts to God and ask him to speak to us in our thoughts as
we read the Bible and particularly the teachings of the Lord Jesus
Christ.

We should also always have a notebook with us and pen or
pencil, and at the beginning of the Quiet Time we should write
down the things we especially needed guidance about for that
day and receive his answers. We should also ask him to explain
the things we read about and meditate on them with him and
make brief notes of everything. Then at the end of the day we
should read over what we had written and check and see if we
had followed the guidance he had given, and if it had really
worked. Or had the results of so doing accomplished nothing to

his glory? If so, we should ask him why this had happened and in what way had we misunderstood his will.

By this means we would learn, step by step, how to recognize his voice and to distinguish the thoughts that came from him from our own self-inspired ones and wishful thinking.

Clarence said that he knew at first it would probably be difficult for us to develop this habit of a daily Quiet Time with the Lord—to be able to wake up early and get up at once. But it was absolutely vital for us to do so by God's grace and power, and if we did we would be eternally grateful for it. He said that a great percentage of the people who yielded their lives to God and then soon backslid into the old self-conscious and self-controlled life from which they had hoped to escape had failed to develop this habit of daily communion with the Lord, talking with him as though they could actually see him present with them. So they failed to receive daily spiritual nourishment and strength, and the newly awakened God-consciousness faded away and vanished.

He told us to look upon these daily Quiet Times as being our greatest and most valuable treasure throughout our lifetime. We were to consider them to be our tryst with the great Divine Lover of our souls; this idea would have a wonderful effect upon our physical bodies and make the development of the vital habit a delight and joy, far more than any tryst with an earthly lover.

He quoted to us a special verse from the Bible and urged us to claim that it would become our own personal experience, so that we too could say with thankful joy, "He wakeneth me morning by morning, he wakeneth mine ear to hear. . .The Lord God hath opened mine ear, and I was not rebellious" (Isa. 50:4, 5 KJV).

Then he told us the story of a man called Old Jo. Old Jo could not read or write. He had been a drunkard who spoke and acted in impure ways, but he had been converted at an evangelistic meeting and had joined a church. His new minister wondered how Old Jo would be able to make progress in the spiritual life, because he could not read a single word in the Bible. But Old Jo soon proved to be a completely transformed character. He knew exactly which of his old ways must be laid aside and what new ones be developed. One day the minister asked him how this wonderful change was being made, and Old Jo told him with a beaming smile that though he himself could not read the Bible, one of his workmates could. This man came to the place where Old Jo lived early each morning on the way to work and read to him a few verses from the Bible about the things that Jesus taught and did. He read them over and over again until Old Jo could say them by heart. Then Jo said happily, "I goes out and practices them all day long!"

Eagerly and thirstily I listened to all these things that night and begged my wonderful new Friend and Savior to make them real in my own experience. So this, the most precious spiritual treasure that I possess, was given to me at that meeting—the God-inspired desire and power to develop the habit of an early morning Quiet Time with the Lord.

I was young, and my stammering mouth had completely prevented me experiencing any trysts with an earthly lover; also I had dreaded waking each morning to face another day of confronting fear and distress and humiliation. I used to cower in my bed as long as possible after waking, putting off to the last moment the need to get up and dress. But from now on, from the very first morning following the day of deliverance from bondage in spiritual Egypt, I claimed the promise in Isaiah 50:4 that the Lord would waken me morning by morning to hear his voice and never let me fail to get up and listen. Oh, glory of glories! He has done just that for sixty-one years. Impossible though it seemed for the first year or two, he not only has never failed to waken me, but also has helped me to get up and take my Bible, Quiet Time notebook and pen, begin talking with him in my thoughts exactly as though I could see him visibly present with me, and to hear him lovingly answering all my questions. It has become a lovely habit and a never-failing joy. I wake morning by morning exactly as though somebody called me or an alarm clock told me that the time has come to wake and get up.

In this way he taught me himself how to begin clearly recognizing which thoughts came from him and which did not. All the thoughts that he inspired were about holy things and desires to know his will and to show his love to others. And all my own thoughts had unpleasant things mixed with them—grumbling, criticizing others, picturing myself in the center of everything, and showing off and wanting others to applaud.

Often, however, when I was seeking his guidance, it was difficult to be sure I was hearing his will or just imagining things myself. For often the things that I thought he was telling me to do seemed so fantastically absurd or totally impossible that I wondered if I was hearing him aright or if I was growing a bit crazy.

But he taught me little by little how to act in such a predicament. Like those described in the Old and New Testaments who believed they heard him calling them to do impossible and foolish things in the eyes of worldly people, I was to take the first step in trying to obey what I supposed he was saying. Then I would ask that if I was not hearing aright, he would block the way and prevent me going any further, or else step by step confirm it and open up the way before me even, if necessary, by working signs and wonders. This often happened. He promised me in the words of the Scripture, "Thine ears shall hear a word behind thee, saying: this is the way, walk ye in it, when ye turn to the right hand and when ye turn to the left" (Isaiah 30-21 KJV).

So I began a completely new kind of life, learning to build daily altars of surrender to God's will and receiving his enabling grace to lay down my self-inspired longings. Looking back over the long years of memory, my life seems to be one bright vista of early morning hours of communion with the Lord, and nothing else seems important in comparison. So life has become more and more a yearning to spend time in the heavenly places with him and his loved ones, even while still here on earth in a mortal physical body. Oh, how inexpressibly glorious it has been!

Soon, of course, I discovered that half an hour or even one hour in the early morning was quite inadequate for these heavenly trysts, and my daily rising hour became earlier and earlier. In the end two or three hours proved to be about as long as my physical body and mind could enjoy without growing weary. But then I snatched moments throughout the day for continuing this lovely communion with him, especially while taking daily exercise in the form of long, happy walks in the country, enjoying the beauties of nature with him and learning to hear him speaking to me and teaching me through all the wondrous forms of creation. I earnestly long that others who read these things will realize how true and wonderful they are and begin to experience them too.

For many people it may be impossible to have their daily Quiet Time with the Lord first thing in the morning. But some special time can, by God's grace, always be fixed during the day and become a blessed habit. So all who long to "grow in grace and in the knowledge of the Lord Jesus" and to know him as the Great Lover and Chief Companion of their lives will be able to do so.

Looking back over the years, I am able to perceive with thanksgiving and love that this daily feeding upon God's word in the Holy Scriptures and writing down in Quiet Time notebooks all the guidance that he gave has been the reason why many years later I was privileged to begin sharing both in books and by word of mouth some of the heavenly manna that he gave day by day. Indeed, it has been his love gift to me; and my greatest privilege and delight has been joyfully to share with others the things that he has taught me and to receive from them the things that he gave to them day by day and in special times of need. Ever since that glorious Passover day from bondage in Egypt to heavenly liberty and joy, which took place at Keswick on July 26, 1924, until this December 1985, he has never failed to nourish and illuminate my heart and mind, and he is doing this all the time to untold multitudes around the world. If someone reading this has not yet begun to experience it too, don't delay. Call upon him and yield yourself wholly to him; enter into the joy of the Lord, which is indescribably glorious and never ending. Like the Children of Israel in the wilderness, begin gathering manna from heaven early, before the "sun dries and the dew melts."

5

The Pillar of Cloud and Pillar of Fire

God led them along a route through the wilderness ... "The Lord guided them by a pillar of cloud during the daytime, and by a pillar of fire at night. So they could travel either by day or night. The cloud and fire were never out of sight."

EXODUS 13:21, 22

THE FIFTH LESSON gave me the key of how to react when confronted with seemingly impossible challenges. For it is by learning to cope with what would be impossible for us to deal with in our own strength that we develop spiritually and learn that we can do nothing really good and satisfying by ourselves. But "with God all things are possible" (Matt. 19:26 KJV.)

So the miraculous Passover escape from Egyptian bondage was symbolically accomplished in my own experience, and a completely new kind of life began. Continually I was challenged to face up to all the things that I felt I simply could not cope with and to find that God's power could change them into priceless blessings and show me how to use them in creative ways.

But everything ahead looked terribly alarming, as, to the delight of my father, I faced the fantastic ordeal of leaving the comparative security of home and going away alone for the first time in my life to study as a student at Bible college, in preparation for becoming a missionary wherever the Lord might choose to send me. But how tender our loving heavenly Father is, especially in his care of those who have been slaves to fear. John Bunyan tells us so beautifully in his *Pilgrim's Progress*, that Our Lord feels very tender compassion for those that are afraid.

During the week after the Keswick Convention, while we still enjoyed the beauties of nature among the Cumberland mountains, our Lord gave me heartwarming and reassuring signs that he would indeed always be with me. One of those confirmations was given the first day after the convention meetings ended. It was a Sunday, and we attended a service in one of the chapels where one of the Salvation Army leaders, Mrs. Booth Clibborn, was the speaker. The subject she chose for her message was exactly the right one for me. She spoke about the lad David who found himself led by God to confront the giant Goliath, who was threatening to destroy him and all the people of Israel. The message was so powerful and compelling and so exactly what I needed to hear that instinctively I leaned forward in my seat in the overcrowded chapel as though every part of my body as well as spirit was stretching out to receive it.

Suddenly she stopped her discourse for a moment, and, leaning over the pulpit, pointed a long, slim finger at me and said, "You there, in that row, you too are confronted by a gigantic seeming impossibility, straddling right across the way before you, making it seem utterly impossible for you to go forward and to do what God is calling you to. But don't fear. Do what David did. He had collected five little pebbles in a pouch, and he took one of them and slung it with all his might straight at the one unprotected place in the giant's armor-covered body—his forehead. The stone bashed right in between his eyes, and the mighty giant fell headlong to the ground. You too must learn to take hold with full assurance of a God-given promise in the Bible, just as David took the pebble. Claim the promise and go forward with the Lord upholding you, and you will find that the impossibility becomes helplessly unable to resist God's will for you or to block the way that he calls you to follow!"

What a perfect message for a "Much Afraid" like me! What a treasure the loving Lord handed to me on the very first morning after the amazing Passover from bondage into a new life!

On the last day before our return home, I walked alone to a high hill near the cottage in which we were staying. There, sitting on the grassy slope, I talked to the Lord as I was learning to do and wrote down in a little book the thoughts and ideas that he gave me. I asked him to speak to me about what looked so fantastically impossible and to help me to begin doing all the things that I had hitherto dreaded and refused to do—like going into shops alone because I could not ask for the things I wanted to buy (and in those days there were no "help yourself" counters) or enrolling as a student in a Bible college or getting into a taxi alone and trying to stutter out where I wanted to go. Of course, I could write down the names of places or articles that I wanted to buy and show them when necessary, but this procedure was appallingly humiliating to my proud nature.

So I talked to the Lord about it and asked him to give me some "pebble" promise to claim just like David. Then, as I sat there alone on the hillside, dark clouds began rolling across a part of the sky, and suddenly, exactly in front of me, appeared a most glorious rainbow, the two ends seeming to touch the ground on either side of me. Never had I seen such a wonderful sight before as that rainbow, placed in such a way that it seemed to shine not only in front of me but above and all around. Then the Lord of Love spoke to me with infinite loving-kindness: "Hannah, this rainbow is my message to you and my covenant promise. I *will* be with you always, wherever you go. I will never leave you, and there is absolutely nothing for you to fear. For my grace *is* sufficient for you, and my strength will be made perfect in your weakness."

So that was his last lovely message as we left Keswick. We returned home and I prepared to launch out into a new life and to start attending Bible college that autumn. Day by day the new, radiant awareness of God's love and his presence with me became more and more real and precious.

We had gone to the Keswick Convention in July. During the month of August I stayed in a little holiday house my parents owned at the seaside a few miles away from the town in which we lived. Throughout that whole month, the Children's Special Service Mission (C.S.S.M.) was holding daily services on the seashore. Happily I attended them, even though I was then nineteen years old. I listened hungrily to all the messages each day. One of them made a lasting impression upon my mind. Not only could I never forget it, but again and again it has challenged and strengthened me during all the years since.

A woman named Miss Bradshawe stood upon the sand pulpit. She held four pieces of white cardboard in her hands and held them up one by one and talked to us about them.

On the first card was printed in big black letters two words that I had used over and over again throughout my life up to that time: "I CAN'T." The next three said, "CAN GOD?" "GOD CAN." "I CAN do all things through Christ who strengthens me."

That was the message we were to take with us, said Miss Bradshawe, and to believe it and claim it in every unhappy situation in which we might from time to time find ourselves. God *can* and does love to help us say about everything, *I can do all things* that God calls me to do through Christ who strengthens me.

Thankfully I took hold of that message and have treasured it ever since. And I can bear radiant witness to the fact that it has been absolutely and unfailingly true all through the past sixty-one years.

My mother had a favorite hymn in the Keswick Hymnbook, which repeats over and over again the assurance that all things are possible to those who believe. See Mark 9:23.

So, armed with my loving Lord's daily messages and assurances and the renewed joy of his presence I prepared to follow him along the impossible-looking path ahead. Autumn came and it was time to pack and get ready for Bible college. I prepared to leave home and to discover in glorious new ways how this wonderful lesson works: that it is only by confronting *impossibilities* in the power of Christ's presence within and with us that we can develop step by step toward spiritual maturity and be able to say with joy and triumph, *"All things are possible* to him that believeth" (Mark 9:23 KJV).

Looking back over the years I find myself wondering if I could at that time have seen the extraordinary adventures, dangers, and challenges that lay ahead, would I not have faltered completely and refused to go forward? Oh, what an amazing, adventurous, and exciting life it has been! But looking back in memory I can only exclaim with adoring thankfulness, *all that he promised he has fulfilled!* He has never failed once. He has never given me a moment's excuse to suppose that he would fail or leave me alone. And so faith learns to "laugh at the impossible" and cry, "It shall be done." And also, "Our Lord is very tender and merciful to them that are afraid."

I am just one of a multitude of adoring souls who bears confident witness to this amazing truth.

6

Crossing the Red Sea

"Don't be afraid.—Just stand where you are and watch, and you will see the wonderful way the Lord will rescue you today. ... The Lord will fight for you and you won't need to lift a finger. ... The Lord opened up a path through the sea, with walls of water on each side; So the people of Israel walked through the sea on dry ground. Then the Egyptians followed them between the walls of water along the bottom of the sea. ... When all the Israelites were on the other side, ... V24 the sea returned to normal beneath the morning light. The Egyptians tried to flee, but the Lord drowned them in the sea. ... V30. Thus Jehovah saved Israel that day ... When the people of Israel saw the mighty miracle the Lord had done ... They revered the Lord and believed in him."

EXODUS 14:13–31

THE NEXT LESSON that I needed to learn was to rejoice over handicaps and infirmities and to discover that potentially they are the most wonderful blessings in disguise. They act as a God-given protection preventing us from becoming entangled in temptations to show off before others. And then, eventually, they turn out to be our greatest means for creative, active work.

So a few weeks passed by at home, and then it was time for me to travel alone to the Bible school in one of the suburbs of the great capital, London, and there seek to prepare myself for work on the mission field. How fantastically absurd and impossible it looked! Now I who had always refused to go into a shop alone because I could not splutter out what I wanted to buy was to set off with luggage to the station and there buy a railway ticket and get into the train. Then when I reached London I was to get into a taxi and try to give the address of Ridgeland Bible College, the Ridgway, Wimbledon, *r* and *w* being the two most difficult letters in the alphabet for me to pronounce!

Wisely, neither of my parents offered to go with me but took the attitude that God told Moses to take toward the frightened Children of Israel: Ex. 14:15 LB. Thus the Lord said to Moses, "Quit praying! and get the people moving! Forward, march! Use your rod—hold it out over the water, and the Sea will open up a path before you, and all the people of Israel shall walk through on dry ground!" So off I went alone, and the loving Lord wonderfully provided. I reached the Bible college, and there I was, started on the way of utter dependence upon the Lord God alone, the one who had so graciously and miraculously made himself real to me.

The staff and students were extremely kind to me as soon as they realized how my speech impediment humiliated me, although it was much less distressingly apparent than it had ever been before. I found I could often say whole sentences without real difficulty. But the principal of the college was guided to help me at once in the best possible way, though I certainly did not agree when I discovered what form it was to take.

As soon as students finished unpacking and settling in, we began studying the schedule of classes, and I found to my horror that every Thursday morning there was to be something called "Speakers' Class." Each week the principal would begin the class by giving some brief teaching on how to become interesting speakers and preachers, able to gain and hold the interest of our hearers and help them to become responsive to the message. When she finished giving us these instructions, three students would then stand up in turn and give a ten-minute talk on any subject the Lord had guided them to prepare. After each of the three had finished speaking the staff and students would kindly indicate their reactions to what had been said and decide whether the talk had been interesting and helpful in some way or not. My name was down on the list of the three students for the second Thursday in the term!

That really was too much. When I realized that I would have to fulfill the assignment, I hurried back to the dormitory where I had unpacked my things. I was desperately determined to pack them again and make my escape and return home at once. I vividly remember standing shaking with terror from head to foot and catching sight of my face in the mirror looking just as it had always done when I was a slave to fear in the spiritual Egypt from which I thought I had just been delivered.

At that moment the loving Lord spoke, and he said in my thoughts, "Hannah, why are you so frightened? Don't be afraid. I really am with you just as I promised to be. At Keswick you told me that you would give me your mouth and let me begin to speak and witness to others through it. So now do just that. Trust me and see what happens tomorrow week at the Speakers' Class, and leave everything to me."

So I put the purse away again and stayed. And later I was grateful that the ordeal was scheduled right at the beginning of the term and was not hanging over me for several weeks of frightened dread.

I settled down to the new life and college curriculum more easily than I had imagined possible. Everyone was kind and helpful, especially the student who slept in the cubicle next to mine and who had been at the college for two terms already. I thoroughly enjoyed the daily classes and, most of all, the fact that every morning early, before anything else started, a bell rang and we students were expected to spend three-quarters of an hour in our cubicles, learning to have a daily Quiet Time with the Lord, just as Clarence Foster had emphasized at the meeting at Keswick. That blessed rule helped me to develop the difficult habit of waking and getting up early in the morning to hold a love tryst with the Lord. This habit has become the greatest blessing in my life.

The terrible Thursday morning arrived, and I was full of fear and the dreadful physical feelings that always accompanied my nervous fears. But I was learning from the Lord that I must disregard all feelings of terror and physical weakness and threatening collapse and simply put my hand in his and go up to the thing that frightened me and discover every time that it was really an immense blessing in disguise. As Frank Boreham says, wise birds know that all the best fruits grow wherever there is a scarecrow, so instead of flying away in fear, they chirp with joy and fly at once to have a rich feast close beside it.

So, impossible as it seemed, I went to the Speakers' Class and sat in the appointed place in the front row with two other nervous students beside me. The principal gave a helpful talk to which I was completely unable to listen, and then she called my name.

There was the Red Sea indeed with Egyptian fears in full pursuit, making a great hue and cry behind me. But at that moment completely new strength was given to me, and I was able to stand up and totter to the platform. I stood there looking out on a room full of embarrassed and sympathetic faces.

And then—there was the Lord himself standing beside me, invisible but gloriously real. And I opened my mouth and said, "The passage of Scripture about which I want to speak this morning and share with you and which I hope will become as real and precious to you as it is to me, is this: *"He said unto me, My grace is sufficient for thee*: for my strength is made perfect in weakness. Most gladly therefore will I rather glory in my infirm-

ities, that the power of Christ may rest upon me" (2 Cor. 12:9
KJV).

Then I said, "You can see for yourselves how true that assurance is, for here am I standing on this platform enabled to speak
to you absolutely freely and without hesitating once, for the very
first time in my life. Oh please praise and thank him with me, as
I tell you about the wonderful way in which he made himself
real to me when I did not and could not even believe that he
existed and I had no faith at all, as I supposed, only a terrified
willingness for him to make me willing to yield myself and my
stammering mouth to him to use as he willed."

Then for ten minutes, without stuttering or spitting once, I told
them about the glorious experience at the Keswick Convention.
Oh, what an atmosphere of praise, thanksgiving, and of immense
relief from embarrassment there was in that Bible college audi-
tiorium! The loving Lord himself spoke to us all and assured us
that no matter how overwhelmingly impossible the coming tests
might be, the Savior promised to give us his enabling grace to
meet them all triumphantly to his glory.

When that Speakers' Class was over, the principal called me to
her and said kindly but firmly, "Hannah, it seems clear that the
Lord wants to use your mouth in a special way. So to help you
to keep yielding it to him, I appoint you to be one of the students
to give a testimony of personal experience at a big meeting to
be held in a slum area in London next week. For the more often
you have the opportunity to open your mouth and to let the
Lord use it, the more quickly you will develop complete dependence upon him and lose your fear of trying to speak to others."

So just a few nights later, I sat perched on a high rostrum in a
large, shabby, almost underground auditorium full of slum dwellers and underprivileged people, many of them enslaved by al-
coholism and impure desires and criminal tendencies. And I was

privileged to speak to them about the glorious power of a real Savior and Deliverer.

And, once again, the miracle happened. I was able to speak without hesitating once, my heart bursting with joy and thankfulness and longing for the loving Lord to help the sorrowful, poverty-stricken people in that room.

When the meeting was over and we returned to the Bible college, one of the senior students came up to me and said, "Hannah, I think the Lord wants me to tell you something that may perhaps be a real help and encouragement to you. I was standing very near the principal at the end of that meeting in the slums, and a woman came up to her and said this: She didn't often go to religious meetings, but as she was passing that mission hall she heard singing and decided to go inside and see what was happening. As she sat down on the back bench a young woman got up on the platform and began to speak and told about the way in which God had been helping her. It was not just what the young woman said that fascinated the person on the back bench but something quite different and extraordinary. It was obvious that the young speaker was feeling very nervous, indeed really frightened at first, but as soon as she opened her mouth and began to speak a whole group of shining, smiling angels gathered around her and seemed to be supporting and helping her in the most beautiful way. The woman reporting this said that she had what were called extrasensory perceptions, which enable her to see many things that are not visible to the physical sense of sight, but she had never seen anything like that before, and she would like the young woman to know what she had seen."

What a beautiful and reassuring message that was! Ever afterward when I had to stand up on platforms to speak—and this began to happen more and more often—that report returned to my memory and reminded me that the loving Savior really was there and also that his shining angelic helpers were all around me, holding back all fear and dread of any kind. And as I discovered with amazed joy, every time I stood up in front of others to speak about the one I love most of all and to whom I owe every lovely and satisfying thing in my life, I could speak fluently and easily, with no difficulty at all. But for twenty-five years the stammer continued to some degree in ordinary conversation, because I did not yet know the cause of it and how it could be completely cured.

So the first term at Bible college passed quickly and happily. There were many tests of different kinds and just as many deliverances, especially at prayer meetings and when I was joining in ordinary conversation. The stammer had lessened but was still apparent enough to embarrass me greatly at times. But it was allowed to continue because I needed it as a protection now that I began to experience, at times, the joy of being able to speak fluently at meetings and the intoxicating delight of finding that this was one of the gifts entrusted to me here in the School of Earth Experience. How easily I could have been snared into showing off before others and seeking gain and glory for myself! Yes, I could so quickly have been corrupted by it. Thanks be to God that for twenty-five years I could never stand up on a platform in order to speak and teach others without feeling that I myself would not be able to say a word, and only the Lord could touch my lips and make me able to be one of his privileged witnesses.

One especially happy thing took place when I returned home at the end of that first term at Bible college. My mother for many years had been a gifted and earnest preacher and Bible teacher, and she continually received invitations to speak in gospel halls and chapels all over the county. She had become ill and could no longer carry out her beloved preaching and teaching work and had begun to explain that she could no longer, because of health reasons, accept invitations. But now what a wonderful joy it was to her to tell those who asked her to speak at their meetings that though she could not go herself, her daughter was now able to take her place!

Lovely opportunities were thus given me to go on witnessing and sharing with others, even during the college holidays. And, most comforting and precious of all, Mother, before she left this earth life, had the joy of seeing the miserably depressed and self-bound daughter whom she had dedicated to God's service while still in her womb now liberated in such a wonderful way and able to continue carrying on her own witness round about our home town.

My mother's illness proved to be her last. Before the end of the second term at Bible college I was called home to be at her deathbed. And there our loving heavenly Father permitted her to give me another blessing and message.

My father, grandmother, a nurse, and I were gathered around the great four-poster bed in my parents' room on which my mother lay, about to breathe her last. She was to all appearances unconscious but occasionally opened her eyes and seemed to look at us. Suddenly her mother looked at me and said, "Hannah, promise your mother that you will stay at home and care for your father and lovingly take her place when she has gone. Make this promise and so ease her mind and do it now."

It is impossible to describe my feelings at that moment. Here was my grandmother urging me to promise my dying mother that I would leave Bible college and give up the whole idea of becoming a missionary and return home to take her place and care for my father! What was I to do? It was too dreadful for words!

Desperately crying in my heart to the Lord for help, I leaned over my mother in an agony of doubt, longing to do the right thing, and said, "Mother! Do you want me to make this promise?"

It seemed impossible that she could answer even if she was, as seemed unlikely, really able to understand me, for she had lost the power of speech. But suddenly, her eyelids fluttered open and she whispered gaspingly, using the old Quaker speech that my parents spoke to each other and to me, "I thought thee had promised the Lord that thee would be a missionary."

"I have! I have!" I exclaimed. "I am already in training at Bible college preparing for that work."

"Then don't let anything hinder thee from being that and doing what he wants thee to do. Thy father wants that too."

Then my mother closed her eyes. Those were the last words that she spoke.

What an unutterable blessing it has been to have had such parents as mine, even though till I was nineteen years of age I couldn't appreciate that fact and caused them both such grief! But their example and prayers and love have been the greatest human influence and enrichment in my life.

7

The Bitter Waters at Marah

Then Moses led the people of Israel on from the Red Sea ... and they moved out into the wilderness of Shur ... and were there three days without water. Arriving at Marah they could not drink the water for it was bitter. "(that is why the place was called Marah, meaning bitter".) "And the Lord showed him (Moses) a tree to throw into the water, and the water became sweet."

EXODUS 15: 22, 23, 25 LB

AFTER TWO YEARS the time came to leave the Bible school and to seek to be shown God's next plan. I had no idea where and in which land he wanted me to be a missionary. I was just twenty-one years old and surely needed more experience in the wonderful new life of union with the will of God before launching out into the deep.

It so happened that in the town where I lived was a man named George Fox, named after the founder of the Society of Friends or Quakers, as they had been called in earlier years. He had been led by God to gather together a small group of men and women who would go out two by two evangelizing in the villages of Great Britain, visiting the places that seemed most remote or where some small chapel or gospel hall had been closed down because of a decrease in attendance. By means of open air services and house-to-house visiting, they sought to revive interest in spiritual things and to get weekly services started again, along with Sunday school for the children.

This group of people was called "The Friends' Evangelistic Band," and their headquarters was quite near my home. I knew the leader George Fox very well and of course had often seen members of the group holding little open air meetings at the street corners. They sang hymns and preached messages that it seemed no one listened to; all hurried past the tiny group, intent on their own special concerns.

During my time at Bible college I had become accustomed to sharing in open air meetings, but those had all been held in a respectable way, mostly on Wimbledon Common, with some well-known minister or evangelist directing the meeting and a large group of well-dressed supporters singing beautiful hymns, accompanied by a trained band of music players. Always a large number of people would gather around, either sincerely interested or merely curious to know what was going on and to enjoy the music.

But to see two or three rather shabbily dressed people standing at a street corner trying to preach the gospel and handing out tracts really embarrassed me. I thought it looked absurd, and I habitually hurried by on the other side of the road to avoid being buttonholed by them or asked to stand in the tiny group that might be there trying to support them. Their witness I looked upon as a useless activity, not what I pictured as being true God-inspired witness. What really glorified him were large crowds listening with absorbed interest to powerful spiritual messages and beautiful music and singing.

So when, soon after leaving the Bible college, a most unwanted idea entered my mind, it came as a real shock. Did the Lord actually want me to join the Friends' Evangelistic Band and gain further training in seeking to attract irreligious people to listen to the gospel message? This idea came to me during one of my early morning Quiet Times as I was thinking about the way in which missionaries must try to attract completely uninterested or fiercely antagonistic people and help them to become willing to hear about the Lord Jesus, the true Savior we all need.

When the idea entered my mind that perhaps some experience working with the Friends' Evangelistic Band might prove a helpful preparation for work abroad among peoples of another religion, I did not like the idea. I talked about it with the Lord and asked to be shown if this unattractive thought really came from him and if I needed the experience of trying to do missionary work in my own home country before attempting it in a foreign land. And the more I prayed, the more my loving Lord seemed to emphasize that it was his will for me to do so.

So one morning I got on the tram in order to go and visit George Fox and ask if he was willing to let me join the band. But, alas, I sat there in the tram feeling superior to the earnest young people who worked with the band and had an upbringing so different from my own privileged one. I was the daughter of well-known, highly respected religious leaders in the town, and I was not a member of the working class, as were all the other young people in the band. Class distinctions were still very important and strictly observed in those days. Moreover, I had studied at a Bible college particularly interested in training members of the upper and middle classes to act as leaders and examples to the working classes in a respectable and God-glorifying way. It fills me with self-loathing and shame now to remember how deeply ingrained in me this superior attitude was. Tenderly but firmly and with great skill, the loving Savior worked to free me from it. And his splendid method was by calling me to work with the Friends' Evangelistic Band.

As I sat there in the tram on my way to ask George Fox if I might join (temporarily, I hoped) his band of absurd young people, my mind was in a turmoil. I remember it vividly, especially some words that flashed into my mind and seemed to sum up all the humiliating things I was tempted to picture. I remembered one of the parables told by Jesus about the man who said, "Behold, these three years I come seeking fruit on this fig tree, and find none: cut it down; why cumbereth it the ground?" Then the gardener said, "Let it alone this year also, till I shall dig about it, and *dung it*" (Luke 13:7, 8 KJV).

"O Lord Jesus," I exclaimed in thought, "how true! Even after two years at Bible college you can see just how I shrink from joining this working-class evangelistic band. Do you mean me to do it? Are you really saying to me, 'This year I will begin to dig about you properly, and *dung* you and help you to become really fruitful'? O Lord, am I to undergo a *dunging* experience so that my horrible pride can be cast down into the mire and dirt in front of everybody?"

Then when I got to that point, all of a sudden I began laughing inwardly, for a God-given sense of humor came to my rescue. I seemed to hear my guardian angel and some of his other angelic friends laughing happily together and saying, "Well now, let's set about digging about Hannah and pouring real rich dung fertilizer all over her and see if we can get her ready for the foreign mission field. What heavenly fun that will be!"

So the interview was held and I was accepted into the band. Once again I found myself entering upon a completely different mode of life from anything I had known before.

The dunging process began at once, and it was a wonderful experience for proud, sensitive, absurdly ignorant Hannah Hurnard. For it proved to be a process of learning to be willing to witness with people who were ready to say, "*We are fools for Christ's sake;* we are weak . . . [and] despised" (1 Cor. 4:10 KJV).

"But God hath chosen the foolish things of the world to confound the wise; and God hath chosen the weak things of the world to confound the things that are mighty . . . And things which are despised, hath God chosen, yea, and things which are not, to bring to nought things that are: That no flesh should glory in his presence. . . . He that glorieth, let him glory in the Lord" (1 Cor. 1:27–29, 31 KJV).

"If any man among you seemeth to be wise . . . let him become a *fool*" (1 Cor. 3:18 KJV).

"He said unto me, My grace is sufficient for thee: for my strength is made perfect in weakness. Most gladly therefore will I rather glory in my infirmities, that the power of Christ may rest upon me. Therefore I take pleasure in infirmities, in reproaches, in necessities, in persecutions, in distresses for Christ's sake: for when I am weak then am I strong" (2 Cor. 12:9, 10 KJV).

The first place to which I was sent as companion to a worker who had been in the band for some years was on the Clee Hills in Shropshire, far away from any town, with not another dwelling place in sight. The cottage where we were invited to stay for several weeks was far away from the lonely country road, and we had to climb three stiles and cross three wide, stretching fields in order to reach it. It was a two-room cottage, with a kitchen and sleeping room and a stepladder in the kitchen that went up to a trap door in the ceiling. In the tiny attic where we could hardly stand up straight were a chest of drawers and one double bed, where my companion and I were to sleep.

What a fantastic contrast it was to everything that I had known hitherto! It was no easy task. I had to adapt to so many discomforts and lack of amenities to which I had been accustomed, including no sanitary arrangements indoors and no water except from a hand pump in the garden. Sputtering candles greeted me instead of electricity; an iron stove burned coal in the kitchen; and a restless sleeper was my bed companion. But the farmer and his wife who lived there were very kind and gave us a happy welcome. They longed to have weekly services started again in the little chapel. There they had worshiped until more and more people left to go work in the town a good many miles away and the chapel had been closed.

Each day we walked long distances and knocked on the doors of all the other scattered cottages, distributing tracts and inviting everyone to attend the meetings we were to hold each Sunday and also on several nights each week. Three or four people did gather the first night and one or two children. I pumped away on an old broken-down harmonium playing the hymns they chose, and my companion did most of the speaking. Daily we stood on any small village green near a group of houses and sang and preached, quite often to no visible listeners except one or two curious cats and dogs, though occassionally we were cheered and spurred on in our efforts when we saw a face peeping out from between the curtains of one or more cottages. Bit by bit things changed, and by the time we left, a handful of people met each Sunday in the chapel and a Methodist circuit preacher began a fortnightly Sunday service and held a class for children.

That was the method we generally used at each place to which we went, but certainly the conditions were not always so drastically primitive and inconvenient as that first location. Indeed, in some villages we were invited to stay in the homes of earnest, well-off Christian people with whom we enjoyed most happy fellowship and generous hospitality. But every place was fascinatingly different, and I must say there was never a dull moment, though many intensely embarrassing and difficult ones!

I was privileged to work and witness in the Friends' Evangelistic Band from 1926 to 1930. Before leaving, I started a little news sheet about the work, which was sent out quarterly to all who were interested. This news sheet has been continued ever since.

I never found the band's method easy to accept and enjoy. I was constantly tempted to leave and join an easier form of witness with fewer discomforts and without the need continually to

appear as "*a fool for Christ's sake.*" I longed for far more spec-
tacular and visible results than seemed possible with the band
work. But nevertheless there were daily joys and blessings of a
very satisfying kind, and certainly, as I discovered later, it was the
best possible preparation for the particular work to which God
would later call me to undertake on the mission field. I now
realize how much I owe to that preparation period in the
Friends' Evangelistic Band.

Looking back on those full years they do seem to coincide
with the record already quoted in Exodus 15:22–26: which tells
us that the people of Israel were led out into the wilderness . . .
and Arriving at Marah (Bitterness) they had been unable to drink
the water because it was bitter . . . Moses pleaded with the Lord
to help them, and the Lord showed him a tree to throw into the
water, and the water became sweet (LB).

That is exactly what I experienced in the Friends' Evangelistic
Band. All the circumstances that tasted so bitter to pride and self-
will became the source of wonderfully sweet and blessed enrich-
ments.

We went continually to what seemed like spiritually desolate,
barren wildernesses all over the British Isles, but again and again
there gushed forth heavenly joy and loving-kindness. Daily we
enjoyed the privilege of feeding together on fruit from "heavenly
palm trees" offered to us in the pages of the Bible, as we read
and studied it together and sought the Lord's messages for hun-
gry, often starving, souls with whom we were brought into contact.

Here in this Book of Remembrance it is a joy to share in the
next chapter twelve lessons and experiences that symbolize the
arrival of the Children of Israel at Elim, where there were "twelve
springs and seventy palm trees." But before arriving at that stage,
the last words about Marah and the tree of new understanding
that I experienced through bitterness is well expressed in Exo-

dus 15:25, 26. "It was there at Marah that the Lord laid before them the following conditions, to test their commitment to him. "If you will listen to the voice of the Lord your God, and obey it and do what is right, then I will not make you suffer the diseases I send on the Egyptians, for I am the Lord who heals you" (LB).

Yes, there were still to be struggles ahead in those band days, with physical weakness such as chronic anemia, tendency to develop feverish chills, and frequent prostrating neuralgic headaches. It was not for another twenty years that I was able to learn from the Lord about the way to begin experiencing this wonderful promise in Exodus 15:26. But I did learn healing for spirit and body there at Marah and began to experience under those primitive conditions that God's grace was indeed able to keep me coping with every difficulty without relapsing back into the old nervous troubles. I began to learn that even with my highly strung temperament I could happily carry on by his grace without breaking down under the strain. Indeed, I became ever more able to overcome physical troubles of every kind and to drink the sweet healing water of his precious promise.

"My grace is sufficient for thee, for my strength *is* made perfect in thy weakness." Yes Lord, how gloriously you fulfilled your promise!

8

The Twelve Springs at Elim

And they came to Elim where there were twelve wells of water and seventy palm trees, and they camped there beside the waters.

EXODUS 15:27 LB

ONE OF THE PLACES where a fellow worker and I stayed for several weeks was a village on the edge of a wasteland stretching for several miles, most of which was covered with thorny bushes and prickly plants. On that thorny wasteland, I took my daily walks with the Lord. For it was becoming a habit to walk alone in the countryside with a little notebook and pencil in my pocket in which to jot down all the ideas that came into my mind as I talked with the Lord.

I once heard someone say that we should never say *why* to God. So I rushed off alone as soon as possible and said to him, "Oh please, *why* must I never say *why* to you?" And the loving answer came. "Ask as many questions as you please, for you will never learn very much if you don't. But never ask God any question with a whine in your voice: 'Why do you let this horrible thing happen to me; it is most unfair and unkind of you.' Always ask with joyful expectation of receiving a beautifully satisfying answer, or as much of it as you are able to receive at the time. The only questions to which you will not get answers are those that it never occurs to you to ask."

So I continued to be a fervent questioner, asking the Lord about his plans and guidance for my daily needs and for his explanations of the Scriptures that I read and studied in my Quiet Times. And the answers became like gathered supplies of spiritual nourishment and water of life for my thirsty soul.

The daily walks on that briar-covered wasteland were not always easy, though they were a constant delight. Often as I followed the narrow tracks between the blackberry bushes or thorny scrub, my clothes got caught and had to be carefully disentangled, and my hands were scratched and bleeding. It was by that means that I learned the first beautiful, spring-of-water lesson: the thorny circumstances of life that prick and hurt us are often God-permitted means to prevent us straying from the path of his will. I was to look upon every jabbing discomfort and lack of material amenities as an opportunity to press closer to his side and to adapt to all such difficulties, not with moans and sighs but with happy assurance that it was permitted in order to keep me from seeking ease and pleasure or aspiring to receive worldly acclaim. I summed it up in these words: *He gives me thorns instead of eyes* so that I shall not be tempted to turn aside from the narrow way and go straying in the broad way, which leads to worldly dangers of all kinds.

The prophet Hosea said of backsliding Judah and Israel that they were like an unfaithful wife who says, "I will go after my lovers, that give me my bread and my water, my wool and my flax, mine oil and my drink. Therefore I *will hedge up thy way with thorns* . . . and then shall she say, I will go and return to my first husband; for then was it better with me than now" (Hos. 2:5–7 KJV).

The message of the second spring at Elim was summed up for me in the words of Isaiah 35. I read them every day and rejoiced over them and claimed them as our Lord's promise to me, too, in those remote villages where there seemed so little sign of real fruit. It was in the second village we went to that this chapter was laid upon my heart.

"Even the wilderness and desert will rejoice ... The desert will blossom with flowers. Yes, there will be an abundance of flowers and singing and joy! ... The desert will become green ... and lovely ... for the Lord will display his glory there. With this news bring cheer to all discouraged ones ... Tell them, Be strong, fear not, for your God is coming ... He is coming ... to save you. And when he comes, he will open the eyes of the blind, and unstop the ears of the deaf. The lame man will leap up like a deer, and *those who could not speak* will shout and sing. Springs will burst up then in the wilderness and streams in the desert. And a main road will go through that once deserted land; it will be named 'The Holy Highway.' ... God will walk there with you. The ransomed of the Lord will go home along that road to Zion, singing the songs of everlasting joy. For then all sorrow and all sighing will be gone forever, only joy and gladness will be there" (Isa. 35:1–2,3,4,5,6,8,10 LB).

How perfectly those verses sum up my memories of those difficult but blessedly happy years in the Friends' Evangelistic Band! God has beautifully given each one of us a Book of Memory. By his grace may we inscribe in it only joyful and blessed things without a single disagreeable or ugly memory hoarded among them. And all the wonderful lessons he has taught us will be safely recorded there forever.

The lesson from the third spring of water was given to me in the words spoken by the mother of our Lord and of all who are members of his body: *"Whatsoever he saith unto you, do it"* (John 2:5). Yes, let us remember never, never to say no to God, but always, "Yes, Father, I delight to do thy will."

A fourth lesson I found myself constantly challenged to remember and respond to with joyful praise and thanksgiving was the lesson I first learned on the shore at the C.S.S.M. service in 1924: "*I can do all things through Christ who strengtheneth me.*"

Day by day in the band work I had to take hold of that assurance, claim it, and prove how true it was during all the adventures of those four years. The loving Lord never failed, though I did again and again. It was then in the evangelistic band that I discovered there must be no compromise of any kind in doing exactly what he told us to do, and no deviating from one single detail of his revealed plan and method. For if we compromised in any way, the blessed experience of doing all things through Christ's strength ceased to operate, and some kind of dismal failure would take place. I found this was the case particularly whenever I was tempted to criticize, blame, or deprecate in any way any of the band members with whom I was assigned to work and who were temperamentally different from me. Failure happened also whenever I was tempted to want to outshine any of them and have more requests to speak and teach at the meetings than they had. Mercifully the Lord demonstrated this principle and let me puncture the power supply and fall crashing to the ground, for always in the case of the Lord's loved children, *pride does come before a fall.*

The fifth wellspring of water at Elim is taught in Matthew 6: "Don't worry at all about having enough food and clothing . . . Your heavenly Father already knows perfectly well that you need them, and he will give them to you if you *give him first place in your life.* So don't be anxious about tomorrow. God will take care of your tomorrow too. Live one day at a time" (Matt. 6:31, 32, 34 LB).

I was tempted frequently in those band days to worry about daily supplies and needs. We stayed in remote places many miles away from shops, and we asked for no salary or payment of any kind except a share of the gifts that were sent to the headquarters house and divided among band members accordingly. Those who invited us to help restart work in the villages where they lived gave us hospitality or gifts of food, and many of them were extraordinarily generous and kind. But in many places they were materially poor, and they were not able to provide everything they would have liked to or for which we would have been thankful. But the Lord himself never failed us, and necessary supplies were always granted, sometimes at the last moment and in truly miraculous ways. So continually the blessed challenge was spoken in our hearts: "He will gladly give you everything you need *if you give him first place in your lives.*"

Yes, that is the golden key. If we stop giving God first place in our lives in some particular way, then increasing shortage of supplies may remind us of this fact. For God does sometimes give give us "thorns instead of eyes."

Then we need joyfully and with absolute honesty to ask him to show us in what way we have stopped giving him first place. Oh, how tenderly and skillfully he does this!

The lesson on the sixth spring of living water was a challenge to *ALWAYS KEEP OPEN TO NEW LIGHT*. Never let us suppose that we have seen the full truth at any stage of our lifetime, because our capacity to see and respond to more light increases all the time. This development in capacity to be aware of spiritual realities depends upon continual willingness to share the light God gives us with others. For if we cease to share the light we shall gradually lose it ourselves. It will fade away and leave us in increasing darkness and weakness and failure.

But the joyful fact is that *light responded to brings us more light*, and that brings us to the seventh Elim spring: we must always share light with others, for when we do that, heavenly light begins to shine around us wherever we go. In Matthew 5:14 we are told that the Lord Jesus said, "You are the world's light—like a city on a hill, glowing in the night for all to see. Don't hide your light. Let it shine for all; let your good deeds glow for all to see, so that they will praise your Heavenly Father" (Matt. 5:15, 16 LB).

As I look back on these pages of memories of the years in the Friends' Evangelistic Band I smile happily at the remembrance of how often it seemed like a waste of time to share the good news of God's love in many of those remote villages. Sunday after Sunday we would go to a little closed chapel now hopefully reopened in order to hold a service. There I would sit at a little pedal harmonium banging out the hymn tunes, and my fellow worker would perch absurdly in the pulpit preaching to perhaps one or two people in the seats—probably our host and hostess, and occasionally one or two more.

But it is never a waste of time to share the light and make it available to others, though it may be that at first we do not always see the best and most helpful ways of doing so. But, praise God, we can learn by experience. I owe much to those day-by-day walks from door to door of cottage homes seeking to talk to others about the love of God and humbly asking to be shown how to do it more and more skillfully.

The eighth spring of living water is learning to look upon humiliations as being real blessings. It is down in the Valley of Humiliation that we do indeed meet with what John Bunyan called the Giant Appolyon straddling across our way and shouting, "Stop! Go no further or I will engulf you in shame and despair!" But Bunyan in part two of his *Pilgrim's Progress* tells us another wonderful thing about the Valley of Humiliation and what a blessed privilege it can be to be called to go down into it. For when we go down remembering that there is only one thing in us that can be really hurt, and that is *pride*, then we find that the Valley of Humiliation can become one of the most fruitful places on the way home to our Father in heaven. For down there "the King has his country house" where he loves to be most of all and to invite his best beloved friends to stay and enjoy themselves with him!

The ninth spring of water at Elim can therefore perhaps be summed up in these words: be willing to learn better ways through our failures, and to have true loving sympathy and understanding with those who slip and fall down into the mire of failure, even public scorn and abuse. So even though there may be

> Many a slip in going down the hill
> Yet for the going down I thank God still.

There were three more springs of living water from which I learned to drink rejoicingly, but they must be recorded in the next chapter.

9

Seventy Palm Trees

(Exodus 15:27 LB)

AT ELIM there were not only twelve springs of water, but also a huge grove of beautiful coconut palm trees, right in the howling wilderness. Only those who know something of desert life can fully appreciate juicy coconuts to eat and drink. And there at Elim, day after day, week after week and, yes, year after year in the band work there was heavenly fruit for us to find and eat with special thrills of joy. We rejoiced over the heavenly fruit and the water at the last three springs.

The tenth spring of Elim water taught a most blessed lesson: when we believe God is calling us to do things that look stupid in the eyes of others, we must obey him and be willing to look like fools. We may be certain of one blessed fact. If we are right in believing he is telling us to do something, when we begin to do it he will confirm it clearly by giving some obvious sign that it really is his will. And if it is not, he will tenderly show us that we were not clearly seeing his will and that there is more for us to learn about receiving his guidance and not our own mistaken ideas. So let us be humbly willing to be shown, when we mistake our own ideas for his, how to avoid doing so in the future.

One precious example of this truth was given to me when I was staying in Ireland, representing the Friends' Evangelistic Band at the yearly week of meetings of the worldwide Society of

Friends, held that year in Dublin. Each day before the special business sessions connected with the work of the Society, everyone attended a period of silent worship together in the large meeting room at the headquarters of the Society in Dublin. We sat there in complete silence, waiting upon God and inwardly and unitedly seeking his guidance and power to control the business of the day.

I sat in the crowded meetingroom beside a kind friend with whom I was staying. The silence was complete. No one spoke or prayed aloud. It was a period of real silent worship, characteristic of old-time Quaker meetings.

Suddenly my friend rose to her feet and stood up alone in that great hushed gathering. I could see and feel that she was trembling from head to foot. But she opened her mouth and began singing. She had a lovely voice, and the words of the hymn sounded clearly all over the auditorium. It was all about the everlasting love of God our Father and the peace and joy of realizing and experiencing that love, and of being able to say with exultant assurance, I am His and He is mine forever.

She sang right through the hymn, which ends with these lines:

> Heaven and earth may pass away,
> Firstborn light in gloom decline.
> But while God and I shall be,
> I am His and He is mine.
>
> W. Robinson

She sat down again, shaking all over. The silence continued unbroken until the time came for the worship meeting to end. The leader gave the signal, and all rose to their feet prepared to go about the special matters on the business agenda.

Then some of my friend's relatives and acquaintances came up to her and expressed great concern and disapproval that she had broken the holy silence in that uncalled-for and most unusual manner. It looked as though she had been trying to show off and publicize her gift of singing.

My friend was wounded to the heart. I tried to comfort her by saying that we should joyfully believe that God had a divine purpose in it or he would not have given her such a strong urge to do something from which she shrank in real humility. Yet the wound continued to be deep and painful. Had she really mistaken her Lord's will and appeared to show off, seeking glory for herself?

Then a day or two later the doorbell rang, and a clergyman stood on the steps. He said that he had come from the hospital, where it was part of his ministry to visit the patients. A couple of days earlier a young man had been carried in after being run over in the main street, and the staff could do nothing for him except try to relieve the pain he was in. He was dying.

The minister knelt beside the bed, and the young man opened his eyes and began haltingly to blurt out at intervals something he wanted to say. "I want to tell you something and to ask your help. I was brought up in a godly family, but I strayed into evil things and became a prodigal and broke my parents' hearts. I never went home again and they are both dead now. I was often sent to prison and finished one sentence just a few days ago. I came out homeless and penniless and roamed the streets looking for something to do or steal. I came to a large building with a sign saying it was the Society of Friends meetinghouse. If anyone needed a friend just then, I did, so I went inside. I found a crowd of people sitting down as though waiting for a service to begin. So I sat down ready to beg from them when the service ended. But no one spoke or moved, and I was just going to get up and leave and start my wanderings again and try to steal something, when a woman suddenly stood up and began singing.

"She was singing just for me, the prodigal son, about God's love for me, even me. As she sang verse after verse, such a sense of God's love and forgiveness filled my heart that I started to cry and could not stop. When she sat down I left, creeping away outside, filled with the certainty that God loved me and was calling me home. When I got out onto the street, a car knocked me over and I was brought here. And now I know with such joy and thankfulness that I am going home.

"Pastor, will you do something for me—the only thing now I really want? Will you go to the meetinghouse and try to find out where that woman lives, the one who stood up and sang for me. Tell her what a debt of gratitude I owe her for being our Father's voice calling me to himself and to his love."

You can imagine the heavenly joy and comfort that message brought to my friend, and the complete healing of her wound. As for me, I can never forget it. Let us share and tell the good news about God's love everywhere and never be afraid of being a fool for Christ's sake.

Another dear Quaker woman opened up for me the eleventh spring of living water. She was in her eighties and had remained unmarried all her life. She had been entrusted by God with a large income, which she tried to spend as he directed. She invited me to spend a few days with her in her beautiful home in England, a large house with many rooms all tastefully furnished and kept in perfect order and condition.

After breakfast on the first morning, she rang a little bell, saying that it was her custom to have morning prayers and a short Bible reading with the members of the staff before they started on their daily housework. When she had rung the bell, in walked eight or nine young maids in starched white pinafores and caps. They seated themselves in a row of chairs, and my hostess opened the Bible and began to read from the Gospel of John. In her beautiful, old but clear voice, she read the words of the Lord Jesus, "*I am among you as he that serveth.*"

I must say that I was completely staggered. How could she dare to sit there and read those words to that row of serving girls? There she was—one rich old woman living alone in a large house, with all of them spending their time waiting on her and carrying out her wishes!

I looked at them to see how they were reacting, and to my astonishment they all seemed to be listening with eager interest and glad response. After they had left the room I discovered why. My hostess explained to me that she looked upon it as part of her God-given ministry to bring young girls from poor homes into her home to train them herself to earn a good living in order to help their poor parents. She taught them how to look after all the beautiful furniture and ornaments as skillfully as possible—all the details of housework and domestic service. Then as one by one they showed that the lessons were well learned and faithfully performed, she recommended them to her friends and wealthy neighbors. They were always eager to find honest and skillful servants to work in their own large mansions and were willing to pay a good wage to them. They all trusted my friend completely, and when they needed extra help in their homes, they applied to her in order to take into their service one of her well-trained maids.

No wonder my Quaker friend felt free to talk to them about the privilege of serving others and doing everything with love and faithfulness and in the best possible way, just as Jesus did himself. Surely by her own example she was saying to those young girls, "I am among *you* as one that serveth. Now I beg you to learn of me to serve in the same heavenly way!"

That same woman taught me the lesson from the twelfth spring of water at Elim. It is a lesson I have already mentioned and which I think is one of the most precious treasures that I possess.

When it was time for me to leave, her chauffeur drove us both to the station, and she saw me and my belongings comfortably settled in one of the railway compartments. Just before the train left she put her head in the window and said in her lovely voice and special Quaker speech, "Hannah, it is a joy to see how earnestly thee loves the Lord Jesus and seeks to obey and serve him, even in ways that must often seem difficult and costly. Here is a special word for thee to remember if thee is ever tempted to feel that the loving Lord asks thee for too costly a sacrifice. Remember this, '*Sacrifice is the ecstasy of giving the best we have to the one we love the most.*'

Then the whistle tooted, the guard waved his flag, and the train moved out of the station. I was left with this lifelong key to ungrudging, joyful service to the Lord of Love himself.

O Lord Jesus! Thank you for these twelve beautiful springs of living water to which I was led during the years in the Friends' Evangelistic Band. And thank you for all the fruit and delicious nourishment from the heavenly palm trees.

10

Food from Heaven in the Desert of Sihn

They left Elim and journeyed on into the wilderness between Elim and Mount Sinai. There too the people spake bitterly against Moses and Aaron. "O that we were back in Egypt," they moaned . . . "Now you have brought us into this wilderness to kill us with starvation." . . . Then the Lord said to Moses, "Look I'm going to rain down food from heaven for them. Everyone can go out each day and gather as much food as he needs." . . . "So They gathered the food [manna] morning by morning . . . (each home according to its need!)." So the people of Israel ate the manna forty years, until they arrived in the Land of Canaan where there were crops to eat.

EXODUS 16

ONE DAY while I was still staying in Ireland, my friend and hostess took me to visit a beautiful spot near Dublin, a little island called "Ireland's Eye." She knew how I loved to walk alone talking with the Lord, and she let me climb alone up a little mountain with a flat top from which a wonderful view of the coast and of Dublin could be seen. It was a real scramble but so lovely when I reached the top. I seemed to be lifted up above earth and to be looking down on it from another realm.

I looked out over the water and began talking to the Lord about the sorrowful situation in Ireland at that time. The tragic enmity between Roman Catholics and Protestants was at one of its peak points, with terrorist activities continually taking place. I had witnessed in a number of the villages and towns in that part of Ireland and also in the western areas, and I had heard about many bitter sufferings. But also I had enjoyed the loving, warm-hearted kindness and generosity of the people when once their trust was gained; they were willing to listen and to respond to the voice of sincere love and friendship.

As I sat there on the top of the little mountain, I opened my Bible and asked God to give me a special message, for it was almost time to leave Ireland and return to England. The Bible opened at the ninth chapter of the book of Daniel, and I began reading. I became more and more arrested by the remarkable way in which Daniel prayed and talked to God about the tragically wrong things happening in the land of Israel, and about the judgments that the backsliding people had brought upon them-selves. How completely Daniel—who had not joined in their cor-rupt practices or violent, destructive activities—identified himself with them and with their sins! Many times he exclaimed to God, "Oh, *we* have sinned and done evil." Twenty-four times he spoke of "*us*" and "*our* sins" and begged for God's forgiveness and merciful deliverance from the anguish and calamity of the Babylonian invasion.

Then I thought of the Irish Friend with whom I was staying and of so many other devoted followers of the Lord Jesus, living day by day in a country torn by strife and filled with hatred, fear, and suffering. Earnestly those lovers of the Lord prayed contin-ually, seeking to be shown how to become peacemakers and healers of incredibly cruel wounds.

As I pondered upon the way that Daniel identified himself so completely with the sins and sufferings of his people and nation, and how the Lord's lovers there in Ireland were learning to in-tercede in the same way, it seemed as though the Lord suddenly spoke to me and said something utterly unexpected: "Hannah, are you willing for me to take you as a missionary to witness in the country once called the land of Israel and now known as sorrowful, war-torn Palestine? Will you identify yourself with the people there just as Daniel did? Will you become one of my witnesses and intercessors in Palestine—the land where I myself lived and witnessed, was rejected and put to death? I am calling you to go there. Will you respond?"

It was a completely overwhelming call. Just the previous year my father, who was chairman and treasurer of a number of different missionary societies, had felt led to visit some of the camps for Armenian refugees in the Middle East. Thousands had fled from the frightful Turkish regime, which had persecuted and almost liquidated the Armenian population in Turkey at that time. He had invited me to go with him and ask for several months' leave of absence from the band to do so. After visiting the Armenian camps he said that we would spend three or four weeks in Palestine, visiting some of the new Jewish settlements to see how they were managing to cope with all the refugees fleeing there from the Nazi persecution in Europe.

I was not at all interested in the modern Jewish settlements and kibbutzim, but the thought of visiting the land where the Lord Jesus himself had lived and done his gracious mighty acts and works of love, and then laid down his own life and risen again triumphantly—that was an absolutely thrilling offer. I had been overjoyed to go.

In some ways I had found that visit unhelpful. The struggle between the Jews and Arabs was already so bitter, and the atmosphere of hate was apparent everywhere. Also what I called the commercialism of the holy places by Jews, Arabs, and Christians alike I had found unattractive indeed. But it had been wonderful to be able on many occasions to get away from the tourist places and to wander alone on the Mediterranean seashore or beside the Sea of Galilee and on the slopes of the

Mount of the Beatitudes, and to listen and commune with the Lord alone in what had been his own earthly home country.

And now here was the Lord clearly and lovingly calling me to go back there—not just to witness to the gospel news, fearfully difficult as that would certainly be among both Jews and Arabs, but also to identify myself with the people as though I were one of them, with no censure, blame, or condemnation of any kind. How could that be possible?

"Lord!" I exclaimed. "Why do you ask me to go there? What is the use? You took me there and let me see the dreadful situation and to meet Jews and Arabs, and you know that I got to a place where I could hardly bear the sight of any of them. What is the use of asking me to try and help people I personally feel it is impossible to love? Instead I feel repugnance at their behavior and methods and actions and their very appearance and facial expressions. Lord Jesus, why Palestine? Why Jews? Why Arabs?"

"Because I was a Jew myself," said the Lord Jesus, "and I suffered there for you and for all the world. Will you go back there, Hannah, and let me teach you how to love those you are tempted to feel are unlovely so that you may become more and more like me?"

Well, what could I say? Only one thing. I knelt down there on the hard ground of the little mountain summit of Ireland's Eye and said, "Here I am, Lord, send me, even horrible unloving me, if that is what you want to do. And I will trust you to do whatever you want and to make me willing and able to let you have your way in my life, even though this looks to be the most preposterous, presumptuous, and absurd thing that you have yet led me to do."

So I went down the little mountain and shortly afterward returned to England. I told my father that I now knew where the Lord wanted me to go and work as a missionary. It was to be in Palestine, witnessing to the Jews.

Then my father looked at me and said quietly, "That is the country and those are the people where thy mother and I dedicated thee to go while thee was still in thy mother's womb, but we never felt free to tell thee where we prayed and hoped that it would be."

Oh, the fantastic marvel of God's ways and doings! And what heavenly power he bestows upon godly parents who truly and wholeheartedly long to know his will and to do it! I owe my father and mother a debt of love and gratitude for their faith and love during all those years when I was such a heartbreak to them. May all God-loving parents rejoice and take courage, and may all wayward, rebellious young people remember thankfully that sooner or later their parents' prayers for them will be answered, just as I myself discovered.

When my father told me that news it seemed to me that in one way it was as though I had never had a real chance to do anything else than what they had so earnestly claimed for me. In a real sense, before I was born I had been "Hooked" by their prayers with no escape from the privilege and blessing of responding to God's will. Oh, glory be to him!

My father was of course wholeheartedly delighted. Many years later he told me that the fact that he had a daughter witnessing in the very land where the Lord Jesus had lived and worked and carried on his mighty saving acts had been one of the greatest joys and satisfactions in his life—the thing for which he thanked God most of all.

But my father was almost the only person who was glad to hear the news and approve it. Almost everyone else was full of forebodings and discouragement; and not surprisingly so. They felt that I was physically and nervously unfit, and that such a highly strung person as myself would inevitably develop another nervous breakdown and be nothing but an added burden to those on the mission field. Of course I was tempted to fear greatly that their warnings would come true. But one thing I feared still more was the dread of losing the consciousness of the Lord's radiant presence with me if I disobeyed the call. I knew that to be bereft of his loving companionship would lead me back into the bondage and hell from which I had escaped six years earlier.

So I went forward and applied to an interdenominational mission we had visited in Palestine. Many difficulties stood in the way of my being accepted. I had no training in any of the kinds of work that the mission carried on in the large medical clinic in the city of Haifa. They were praying for qualified nurses and medical helpers and also for a competent secretary, and I knew nothing about any of those skills and had only had four years in evangelistic work. But they had two evangelists already and did not feel they needed another one, certainly not a woman evangelist to orthodox Jewish people, who would be outraged at the very idea. Also, my health record was certainly not good.

So time passed with no definite decision, until at last it was decided that I could, if I wished, go as a voluntary unpaid or honorary worker willing to do any odd jobs that no one else had time for. Following my father's suggestion and request, I was to be free to return to England for two months' rest and recuperation during the time of climatic adjustment. Then it would be seen if my health could be maintained. My father would pay the travel expenses.

Was ever a more ignominious arrangement decided upon! But it was arranged. Even then I, with absurd naivete, did not in the least realize how some of the other missionaries would feel about having such an addition to the staff—an honorary member with special privileges and no particular work to carry out. But in January 1932 I arrived in Palestine and was received at the mission station on the lower slopes of Mount Carmel. Yes, it was the very mountain described in 1 Kings 18, the chapter that in 1924 I had read about how the prophet Elijah called down fire from heaven. Then all the people shouted and cried, "The Lord, he is God! The Lord, he is God!" In a spiritual sense, the same experience had happened to me, and I had begun a completely new life in union with God. What incredibly fantastic and wonderful things he chooses to do! Truly his ways are past finding out. "He is altogether lovely" and wonderful beyond words.

11

Massah

Now at God's command the people of Israel left the Sihn desert, going by easy stages to Rephidim [meaning to spread out wide]. "But upon arrival there was no water. So once more the people growled and complained to Moses. 'Give us water!'" they wailed. Tormented by thirst, they cried out, "Why did you bring us here to die with our children and cattle too?" Then Jehovah said ... "Lead the people out to Mount Horeb (also meaning desert). I will meet you there at the rock. Strike it with your rod ... and water will come pouring out, enough for everyone." Moses did as he was told and the water gushed out! Moses named the place Massah—("meaning tempting Jehovah to slay us"), ... Sometimes they referred to it as Meribah—(meaning "argument" and "strife")—for it was there that the people of Israel argued against God and tempted him by saying, "Is Jehovah going to take care of us or not?"

EXODUS 17:1–7

ARRIVING ON THE mission field felt like coming to a desert place. I so longed to serve the Lord and to be of use to those already on the staff, and I quickly found that seemingly there was nothing that I could do to be of real help.

I was in a place where I could not speak any of the languages used by the people of the land, where the climate and daily work were drastically different from what I had been accustomed to, and where everyone was a stranger. It felt like an overwhelming situation. My body, which was not very strong at any time, had difficulty coping with the heat and humidity on the shore of the Mediterranean Sea and the sudden stormy winds and torrential rainfalls. I felt utterly exhausted all the time, for I was still chronically anemic, and could find no rest even when lying down at night. My body felt too heavy for the bed, and I would toss and turn and get out and walk about to ease the pain of intense cramp.

My room was on the top floor of the main mission house, in an apartment with two trained deaconess nurse sisters, one from Germany and one from Finland. They knew very little English. But they were kind indeed. They worked with the mission doctor at a large daily clinic in the town of Haifa, where my first experiments in trying to help were to be made. The founder of the mission had recently died, but his wife carried on the supervision of the work in a most wonderful way. She lived in an apartment downstairs, and we ate our meals with her. An Arab woman helped in the kitchen and did the housework, and it was difficult to communicate with her too, as I did not know a word of Arabic.

The clinic was quite a long way from the mission house, and in those days there were still no proper roads and no automobiles. The sisters drove to the clinic each day (and I went with them) in a two-wheeled carriage pulled by a hired horse, while the doctor rode on horseback. The other helpers in the clinic, as well as members of the mission staff, lived in another house, and the evangelists in their own homes.

Very soon it became quite plain that as I was completely untrained in medical things and could not easily understand the sisters, I was more of a trouble than a help. So I was appointed to sit in a waiting room at the clinic and give English classes to all who might like to attend the lessons. The reading book was to be the English Bible, because the free classes were offered by a Christian mission. But soon complaints were made that the

Bible language in the Authorized Version (and there were no modern translations in those days) was so different from everyday speech that it was more or less useless; so my task was certainly not an easy one. Many young men and women, both Jews and Arabs, greatly wanted to learn English in order to be able to obtain better-paid jobs with the British mandatory government, and I had no difficulty in finding pupils, only in holding their interest and helping them in the way they wished. I was led to devise a happy scheme whereby we started each lesson by reading together a few verses in the Gospels, haltingly talked about them, and then switched to ordinary reading books. That seemed to be more and more satisfying to all concerned. For I too found those classes helpful, picking up more and more of the Hebrew language and practicing what I was learning twice a week from a Hebrew teacher. I also learned to speak a little of what was called "kitchen Arabic." The mission staff exhorted me to make the best possible use of this opportunity to become more fluent in Hebrew, to be able to read the Bible in that language and give Bible lessons and Christian teachings to a number of pupils who were not patients.

Sometimes, if one of the medical attendants or nurses was not well, I was asked to do simple work in the clinic such as washing the utensils and helping to sterilize them. But one hot day, being intensely thirsty, I misread the label on a big jar and took a gulp of undiluted colorless disinfectant. That was nearly the end of my missionary efforts, for though the sister in charge immediately caused me to vomit up all that I had swallowed, it had burned my interior, and I quickly developed serious jaundice and had to spend several painful weeks in the hospital at Nazareth. But that too turned out to be a great blessing, for there I got to know the truly Christlike Scottish doctor who was the superintendant of that work, and also the matron and several of the nurses. Fellowship with them and later with the staff at the mission hospital in Tiberias beside the Sea of Galilee became a joyful experience. But that particular episode did end all efforts to make me useful in the clinic! It was fortunate that my father had arranged for me to spend two months of each summer during the greatest heat period at home in England, for there I was able to relax and recover from the stresses and strains on the mission field.

I must bear happy witness to the fact that the medical sisters and those I lived with were kindness itself and very patient. But it was not easy for members of the staff from other European countries to enjoy happy fellowship with me. I discovered this soon after my arrival, when one of them felt constrained to exclaim, "Do you know what we call you behind your back? We call you, 'The proud Miss Hurnard.'"

I was hurt and shocked at such an unjust verdict. How could I be proud when I left my home country and had come to work among poverty-stricken Jews and Arabs, almost all of whom were still practically illiterate, and was trying to serve them as best I could? But when I talked to the Lord about it, he said gently, "But you know, Hannah, it is true." And he drew my attention to a lifelong secret habit. I used my imagination in a proud and conceited way, picturing myself doing all sorts of wonderful and highly spiritual things, while others looked on admiringly—or jealously. Always I was the center of the picture; indeed often I saw myself as one of the most spiritually minded missionaries in the Middle East, which I earnestly wanted to be. "That was how the proud Miss Hurnard materialized," said the loving Lord, for "as a man [or woman] thinketh in their heart, so they are." What a tremendous and humbling challenge that was!

On another occasion, one day during my free time, I was floating blissfully on my back in the blue waters of the Mediterranean in the bay of Haifa. Suddenly another body floated near, and a man's voice I recognized as a member of the staff said, "In some ways, Miss Hurnard, you would make an excellent wife, but you would have to marry a poor little man who did everything you told him."

I was so furious I swallowed water and sank like a stone to the bottom. By the time I came up sputtering, the other body had floated away. What a wonderful blessing a sense of humor is! Often I have laughed happily to myself over that unasked-for comment and thanked the Lord that some poor little man had a fortunate escape.

Yes, I had much to learn during those first few years and many difficult adjustments to make. I still hesitated in speech quite badly when I felt tired and strained, which seemed to be most of the time. I certainly let things get on my nerves in a dreadful way, though I repented continually and thirsted and longed to do better and begged the Lord for his help. It was a real Massah and Meribah experience for four long years.

But too there was always living water "gushing from the rock." The daily early morning Quiet Times never failed to bring it in abundance, and communion with the Lord became closer and more precious than ever before.

During those first four years it sometimes looked as though the doleful warnings given in England would come true and that I would be permanently invalided home. But it never happened! And I learned one precious and wonderful lesson during that period—one of the most helpful ones in the whole of my Christian life—which will be recounted in the next chapter.

12
The Amalekites

Then the warriors of Amalek came to fight against the people of Israel at Rephidim. . . . So Joshua and his men went out to fight the army of Amalek. Moses, Aaron and Hur went to the top of the hill. And as long as Moses held up the rod in his hands, Israel was winning; but when he rested his arms at his sides, the soldiers of Amalek were winning. . . . Moses' arms finally became too tired to hold up the rod . . . so Aaron and Hur rolled a stone for him to sit on, and they stood on each side holding up his hands till sunset. As a result, Joshua and his troops crushed the army of Amalek.

EXODUS 17:8–13

DURING THOSE FIRST YEARS in Haifa on the slopes of Carmel, there were continual outbreaks of Arab terrorist activity in Palestine, and they grew worse and worse. The extremist Arab groups sought to prevent the increasing influx of Jewish refugees seeking asylum from the Nazi massacres in Germany. At the same time, thousands of poverty-stricken Arabs from surrounding countries also moved into Palestine to obtain work under the mandatory government. They built roads and worked in any kind of job they could find, but without passports or permission to do so. They claimed that since Palestine was part of the Arab territories, they had the right to enter. Continually there were outbreaks of violence, sabotage of Jewish property, snipings, and exploding land mines. Trains were blown up and derailed, and the most cruel happenings became commonplace events. Then retaliation methods by the Jews began and continued, over the years.

As a result, the atmosphere seemed to be soaked in hatred and desire for revenge. It became more and more difficult to cope with one's own feelings of shocked horror and loathing at what was going on. Constantly I was tempted to feel bitter hatred at all that we had to witness and hear about day by day.

A Christian British policeman working with the mandatory government often came to services at the mission chapel. One day he described to me his own shame and horror at the feelings that more and more often filled his heart. "Miss Hurnard, when you have seen a truckload of your own companions and friends drive over a road mine with everyone in it blown to pieces, and you have had to pick up the hand of a comrade here, and a leg there, and parts of a head and shattered bones scattered every-where, it feels exactly as if hell opens before you, and there is only one desire in your heart—and that is to stop the next car-load of Palestinian people, Jew or Arab, and compel them to drive over a land mine in just the same way."

I knew just how he felt. The temptation to want those in au-thority to give terrorists their own treatment was sometimes ter-ribly strong. It was easy to refuse to remember the teachings of the Lord Jesus and to wish for complete vengeance on the de-stroying forces so rampant in the country, instead of practicing compassionate, forgiving love.

But other situations besides physical terrorism are also pain-fully difficult to forgive and forget. And one day news came of tragic injustice, scandal, and false accusations against persons with whom I and others were closely associated. This news, com-ing on top of the daily tests in the clinic and the strain of the surrounding terrorism finally had an effect on my health. I picked up a virus and lay on my bed tossing with a fever.

One day a knock came on my bedroom door, and a woman I did not know stepped up to my bedside. She said ever so kindly that she had heard that I was undergoing a severe test that I felt to be very bitter indeed. God had laid it on her heart to come and see whether she could help me find a victorious and God-glorifying solution to the problem.

There was something so gentle and understanding about her expression and tone of voice that, stranger as she was, I found myself pouring out the whole matter to her. Then I finished with a desperate cry of shame, "I know I ought to be able to forgive those who are acting in that unjust way but I can't do it. It seems impossible!"

My unexpected visitor smiled at me and said happily, "Now I know just why the Lord told me to come here. For I can tell you the golden secret of how to become able to love and forgive those who are acting wrongly, and even to forget all the grievous details instead of brooding on them and making the pain worse."

I lay on the bed and looked at her and said to myself, "Oh yes, it's easy for you to say and feel that yourself, but this thing hasn't happened to you. If it did I guess you would feel just as I do!"

She must have seen the expression on my face, but she went on gently. "Just take the whole of this unjust situation to the cross of Jesus and ask him to forgive the wrongdoers and your own resentful feelings. Yes, ask the Lord Jesus to forgive all of you—everything that he sees is unloving and evil."

"Oh!" I exclaimed. "Of course I know that, and I have done it a hundred times over. But it just doesn't work. I still can't feel forgiving, and it's going on all the time, so naturally I can't forget it either."

She smiled again and said gently, "You didn't give me time to finish giving the whole prescription. When you have asked the Lord to forgive everything, lay the whole matter down at the cross and leave it there, and promise the Lord that by his grace you will never mention the matter again to anyone or to yourself in thought. Then you will find not only that all your unforgiving feelings fade away completely, but also that you will be able to forget all the bitter details, as though they no longer exist but have become blessings."

I confess I did not believe what she said, but I was in despair, so I decided to ask for God's grace to test it. Whenever friends sympathetically asked about the difficult situation I just said, "Please excuse me, but I have promised the Lord that I will never speak about it again. I am only to bless everyone concerned in it."

After the first few difficult attempts, it worked like holy magic. Quite soon the bitter feelings seemed to be disappearing, my body felt better and better, and the fever left me. And lo and behold, all sorts of completely new and happy, things began blossoming around me and also in the circumstances of some of the others involved. The seemingly unjust and bitter occurrence began to be transformed and actually brought blessings, peace, and contentment, along with grace to bear it happily.

As I look back on those pages in the Book of Memory, it seems to me that the kind visitor was led by God to teach me one of the greatest heavenly secrets of all. Never should we talk about unlovely and wrong things that others do, but instead we are to take them to the cross and ask for God's forgiveness for our own resentful reactions and for his mercy on those doing the wrong things. Then we can leave it all at the cross as though it had never happened, and so it can do no real harm at all. Thank God for such a golden key!

Nearly four years passed while I lived in Haifa, helping in any way I could. I taught English and at the same time learned Hebrew without realizing what a storehouse of treasures that language was going to open up to me in the future. Then, once again as I prepared to spend two months with my father in England, the time approached for another tremendous challenge and the opening up before me of a new door of opportunity.

I made the visit, and on my return to Haifa I found that changes were taking place in the clinic. New staff fully trained in medical work had arrived, but the Arab man who had acted as doorkeeper controlling the entry of patients into the doctor's consulting room was now needed for other work, and I was asked to become the doorkeeper in his place.

What a job that was for "the proud Miss Hurnard" who was learning to long wholeheartedly for some real means of being more helpful in the mission work! This new service did not need medical knowledge, but it certainly did need patience and grace to a degree greater than anything required of me before.

Daily over a hundred poor, illiterate men and women and little children crowded into a big hall used as a waiting room, and a short gospel service was held. On arrival each patient was given a card with a number on it which they had to show when, after the service, I called that number. It was then their turn to enter the doctor's consulting room and not before. But each one wanted to go in as soon as they arrived and not have to sit waiting, perhaps for a couple of hours, until their turn came. They jostled and pushed each other; they argued and pleaded; the babies wailed and the children fidgeted and squabbled; and certainly God-given patience and grace were needed to maintain order and as far as possible an atmosphere of peace and friendliness, as befitted a Christian place of succor and mercy. It seemed to me that superhuman effort was needed and only the Lord of Love himself could give it.

Day by day, in a wonderful way, he really did help, and no uncontrollable uproar or physical violence broke out. Certainly, I began to realize that this kind of training in self-control was just what I greatly needed. And I was able to thank God for it, though, alas, I did over and over again fail to some degree and express impatience and bad temper.

During one period of time a patient came daily whose behavior seemed impossible to cope with. He always arrived late, after everyone else was seated, and so he had to sit at the end of a long queue of waiting patients. But he always insisted with loud outcries that he must be admitted to the doctor's room at once. He would push others aside and even kick them, and of course they kicked and pushed back. But finally he would work his way to the door of the doctor's room where I was sitting or standing, and I often had to intervene my white-coated body between him and the door to prevent his banging on it, and to face his waving arms with quiet, steadfast immobility.

One day this man arrived in what seemed to be an uncontrollably threatening mood. All the other patients grew furious with him and with me for not dealing with him firmly enough. At last he reached the doctor's door where I stood pressing myself firmly against it to bar his way. He hissed and snarled at me threateningly and raised his voice in loud shouts. Then I lost my temper and loudly angrily rebuked him. How dared he speak and behave in that way to me, an English woman like those in the mandatory government? Who did he think he was with his absurd, impertinent demands?

Suddenly the key turned in the door behind me. It opened, and I nearly fell backward into the doctor's arms. He quietly said to me, "Let him come in, Miss Hurnard, I will see him now." Then he put out his hand, took the man's arm, and drew him into the room, as the patient leered at me in triumphant glee. Then the door was again closed and locked.

I was furious with the doctor. He had undermined my authority in front of all the waiting patients watching my humiliation, and he had made it impossible for me to maintain law and order. I felt like banging on the door and shouting in English that I was leaving immediately and would never enter the clinic again. The proud Miss Hurnard was ready to expose herself for all to see.

But then the loving voice of the Lord began speaking to me, and he said, "Oh Hannah, that poor man whom I love so tenderly and all those other patients did not see me standing here among them, did they? They were not shown how I long to help and comfort them, and that this clinic is opened to them in my name and they are invited to come here and meet with me. What kind of thoughts will they have about me when they see and hear you, one of my representatives, acting and talking in the way you did?"

I was overwhelmed with shame and sorrow and horror at my behavior. I had utterly failed to let the loving presence of the Lord and Savior be felt instead of the haughty, furious "lording-it-over-others" behavior of the foreign British woman. In anguish I cried to the Lord to help me and to show me what to do.

Presently the door opened and the man came out, still leering triumphantly. At once I was helped to say, "Oh, I do want to tell you how sorry and ashamed I am that I spoke to you in that way. This clinic where you all come every day belongs to the Lord Jesus, who wants to show you all how God loves you and longs to help you in every possible way. Please forgive me and never, never suppose that the Lord Jesus would have spoken to you as I did."

Everyone was listening, for the first time in complete silence. To my amazement the man burst into tears and gasped out, "Oh, I am so ashamed of myself that I behaved in that way. I hate myself every day for acting like that, but I just can't help it. I am covered from head to foot with an itching skin and cannot sleep or rest all night, and I go crazy until I can get into the doctor's room where the nurses cover me with soothing ointment to ease the itch and give me a few hours' rest. I am so ashamed."

So there we stood looking at one another and understanding one another in a completely new way. Friendliness and sorrow shone out of his eyes and out of mine too. Now I understood how he felt and why he compulsively acted in that difficult way, and I so blindly and hardheartedly had never realized it before.

It seemed incredible, but from that day we were friends. Then and there the other patients also relaxed and began talking to one another in a friendly way, and it seemed as though a miracle had taken place. And it really had. From that day, whenever that man arrived we greeted each other warmly. He smiled at me happily and was given wonderful control over his nerves. Indeed, it seemed that he was responding in a new way to the treatment given by the doctor and the sisters, and his skin was being healed.

What a wonderful new lesson I learned through that experience! Never should we judge or blame anyone in thought or word for anything they say and do but ask the Savior's help in imagination to become that person—to put on their clothes, as it were, and picture their circumstances and temptations. And if we ask the Lord's grace and help to love and have compassion on them just as they are, he will be able to give them real help through us. By becoming the other person, just as our heavenly Father does, perfect understanding of how to help in the best and wisest way will be granted to us. Remember, we are told that it was when "Jesus was filled with compassion" that he was able to heal the sick and to succor the needy. That is the real secret of how to transmit our heavenly Father's power and grace to others. Have compassion on all who stray, and never condemn anyone.

So that was my experience of Amalek—the temptation to attack and use force—and how it was overcome and changed into loving sympathy. It seemed as though that experience and the beautiful lesson taught to me were signals preparing me to follow the Lord through another open door into the real purpose for which he had called me to Palestine. For soon the Arab doorkeeper was free again to take over that work, and I was able to go forward where the Lord led into a realm of completely new work and witness in the Holy Land.

13

Jehovah Nissi, the Lord Our Banner

Moses built an altar there and called it "Jehovah Nissi" (meaning "Jehovah is my flag"). "Raise the banner of the Lord," Moses said, "For the Lord will be at war with Amalek, generation after generation."

EXODUS 17:15, 16

I FIND IT helpful to think of all the enemies in the Old Testament as symbols of our different temptations, which have to be overcome by God's grace and changed into positive Kingdom of Heaven attitudes and behavior. The name *Amalek* means trouble, mischief, and punishment pronounced upon all that causes harm to others. The Amalekites were "dwellers in low places," and God our Father is indeed determined to rescue us from acting in any less than the highest possible good way, for he is the "Most High God."

One morning each week the whole mission staff met together for a prayer meeting. Each person gave a short report on the week's activities; then everyone discussed and prayed over the needs and problems together.

Soon after the new skilled helpers had been given their clinic assignments, the Arab evangelist reported on his visits in Arab villages around Haifa and remarked sadly that there were so many, many villages and Jewish settlements all over Galilee where no visits were ever made and no gospel witness given.

Travel was difficult in those days, with so few roads and hardly any automobiles, and thus the more distant villages remained inaccessible. Also, during the rainy season the dirt tracks even to nearer places were waterlogged and impassable.

During all the long years of Turkish rule until the time of the British mandate, all travel had been by donkey or mule or on camels or in two-wheeled carts drawn by a horse. Now, however, new roads were being built, and a few automobiles were appearing. There was still nothing but a rough, narrow donkey track up the slopes of Mount Carmel, and no road connected Haifa and Acre, except along the seashore at low tide, through soft shifting sands in which an automobile was prone to sink and remain stuck. However, a new road was just in the process of being built between these two busy port towns. But there were no Christian workers available for evangelizing further afield, so that all missionary work was concentrated in the towns. Village people had to seek medical help there, obliged to make long, difficult, and exhausting journeys by donkey. And there were no churches except in the towns.

Just at this time the mission staff rejoiced in the purchase of a new automobile; one of the few seen on the dirty, untarred streets. The doctor was now able to drive the sisters to the clinic, though it was still necessary to hire a horse or donkey to go up Mount Carmel to visit the friends at the German mission on the summit when they needed medical help.

After the evangelist had given his report on the need to witness in the villages and not just in the city, we gathered in prayer for all the mission needs. During that time the Lord suddenly and unexpectedly spoke to me. He said that the time had now come to start the work he wished me to do in Palestine and for which I had trained in England. In Haifa there had been time for me to learn to speak the Hebrew language—though I never became fluent—and now I was to begin visiting Jewish villages and settlements in that part of Galilee where neither the Arab nor Jewish evangelists were able to go. Bibles and New Testaments were to be taken to each place and distributed freely. I was free now to begin this work, and it was exactly what I had been trained to do.

It was an overwhelming challenge, and it looked utterly impossible. I said nothing at the prayer meeting, but when it was over I slipped away alone and talked it over with the Lord on the thornbush-covered slopes of Mount Carmel. Earnestly I begged to be shown his real will and not to be snared into some crazy, self-inspired action. I went through the impossible-looking difficulties one by one and asked for the Lord's answers.

1. How could the outlying settlements and villages be reached from Haifa? They were too far away and I would have to sleep somewhere, and certainly no one would want to take me in, despised Britisher as I was and a missionary.

Answer. Roads were now being built all over the district, and more and more places were within reach by automobile. These were to be visited first. Meanwhile, more roads would be made and more places become accessible.

2. But surely I could not go alone.

Answer. No. I must seek the help of other missionaries, and we were to go two by two to every place just as the first followers had been told to do by their Lord and Master. That was the method he himself had instituted for spreading the gospel news.

3. But what were we to do when we got to the villages? How were we to witness uninvited to people who were violently antagonistic to the gospel message and to all Christian missionaries?

Answer. We were to do just what I had been trained to do in the British Isles: to go from door to door and knock on each one and try to speak to individuals about the good news of the gospel of Jesus Christ.

4.   But I did not know Arabic.

Answer. No. But the Arab evangelists were beginning to hear the call, and they would go to the Arab villages, and others who could speak Hebrew and German (and I knew both) were to begin going to the Jewish settlements, knocking on the doors and speaking to individuals wherever they could be found.

5.   But many of the Jewish settlements were run on communal lines, and there were no separate houses but big dormitories and rooms where everyone met together. So how could we go from door to door and escape being chased away by large groups of indignant people?

Answer. We would be shown God's plan for that kind of visiting a little later on. Meanwhile, we were to start with the settlements where there were individual homes.

6.   But Jewish people who were immigrating into Palestine by the hundreds of thousands, escaping from the Nazi atrocities in Europe, hated all Christians and the Christian teachings, because it was in Christian countries and at the hands of Christians that they were suffering such awful persecution and had done so for many centuries. They would certainly reject our message, slam the door in our faces, and drive us away at once with no opportunity given to us to talk to them. And they would tear the New Testaments to pieces.

Answer. We were to seek God's enabling grace and guidance, and he would show us just what to do as soon as we were willing to begin.

7.   But I was a woman, and such work surely needs men. Orthodox Jews would be still more outraged and insulted if a woman went to them in order to propagate the hated Christian teachings.

Answer. There were many lonely Jewish housewives in those isolated places who would be thankful to have kind women visit them, especially if one of them was a trained nurse. So the first places we were to go to were to be those where patients lived who had been helped in the clinic. They would be happy to see and welcome us. Since each patient who came to the clinic had been asked to give their address, records had been made.

8.   What about the dangers of two women going about alone? Rape, violence, murder, and robbery were commonplace in those days, and no one traveled anywhere alone or without some kind of protection.

Answer. Our motto and safeguard was to be the verse in Psalm 20:5. We were to "lift up a banner of witness" to the Lord Jesus and he and a host of ministering angels would be round about us protecting us, and no evil of any kind would befall us.

So there on the prickly sheep track between thorny bushes on the slopes of Mount Carmel, I received my instructions and knew that, in spite of impossible-looking difficulties, a start was to be made and I was to do it.

It so happened, under the Lord's perfect timing, that this tremendous challenge came to me just as I was due to start for my two-month summer visit to England. So I said nothing before I left a few days later. But when I got to England I told my father all about it. He was filled with joy and enthusiasm (he had no imagination and never pictured possible dangers), and to my awed delight he bought for me a little Austin car which I was to take back with me to Palestine and use to begin the visiting work in the settlements around Haifa where there were already roads.

When I returned to Haifa with the little car I talked to the doctor and sisters about the idea of visiting the settlements where past patients lived who had heard the gospel message preached at the daily services in the clinic before the medical work started. The doctor and the sisters all liked the idea of being able to keep in touch in that way and do some follow-up work. So it was decided that twice a week one of the sisters in uniform would go with me in the little car to experiment with this work of seeking to evangelize outside the city.

That was how it began. Twice a week one of the sisters and I got into the little car, and we drove off along a newly made road or over a bumpy earth track, praying to be protected from land mines and snipers, to visit the new settlements in the Haifa area and the Bay of Acre. First we went to the houses of clinic patients, and generally we received a warm if shy welcome, for unfriendly, anti-Christian neighbors would be looking on. Then, tremblingly and prayerfully, we ventured from door to door in some street where we knew no one, trying to talk to complete strangers. There were mixed results, but always we received at least one or two lovely encouragements. Then we would drive back to Haifa in the little God-given car, bursting with a mixture of relief that the difficult, often dangerous ordeal was over, but also with the joy of the Lord singing in our hearts in a way that we had never before experienced.

After that beginning, step by step the way opened before us. I was able to contact other missions working among Jews, and each week one of their workers would be freed to go with me. Soon I was busy five or six days a week. Then God provided another full-time companion and a second car for her to use, and after poring over a map of all the villages and settlements together, she would drive off to visit in one area with a companion, and I would do the same in the other car. We were given wonderful free supplies of Bibles and New Testaments, donated by Bible societies and other groups. We continued the work year after year, going further and further afield and sleeping at different mission stations while we visited in their areas. We believed that distributing thousands of Bibles and New Testaments in this way was like placing holy spiritual dynamite in strategic places, preparing for the time when the Holy Spirit would light the fuse and cause a tremendous outburst of spiritual revival all over the country among both Jews and Arabs.

This work began in 1936 and continued until 1947 with no interruptions. The Second World War broke out in 1939, and since the Mediterranean was closed to shipping and air travel was too dangerous, for eight years I was unable to visit England again. How wonderful it was that the little car was donated while it was still possible to transport it to Palestine!

The years passed, and all over the country terrorist activities grew worse and worse, as Jewish terrorists sought to force the mandate to be ended. Eventually no cars were allowed to drive about except with an armed convoy, and then none but V.I.P.'s were granted licenses and permits to drive their cars. But I was granted the special privilege of being allowed to continue driving all over both Jewish and Arab areas in the country until every place had been reached. Two of the gift cars did have to stop driving about, but not until every place was reached did I have to lay aside the little Austin car. I never drove in convoy, as my Quaker principles did not allow me to do that. The Bible women and mission workers who went with me knew that often armed Arab terrorists were listening to the messages given by the Arab Bible women in the public square or village gathering place, but we were never molested. One other woman was allowed to continue driving about; she was a government social workers in the Nablus district, but in the end she was shot dead. Another woman friend of mine returning from a church service was also shot to death. But truly the angels of the Lord were round about us, and though more than once bullets were fired at us, none hit, and the car did not receive any kind of damage. Glory be to the Lord, who called us to lift up a banner of witness in his name. "*Jehovah Nissi!*"

This book is written with only one purpose in mind, that is to share with others some of the glorious outstanding lessons taught to me in the School of Earth Experience. In the next chapter I want to write about one of the most beautiful and life transforming insights of all.

14

Jethro, the Priest of Midian

"Word ... soon reached Jethro, Moses' father-in law, the priest of Midian, about all the wonderful things God had done for his people and for Moses. Then Jethro took Moses' wife Zipporah to him, ... along with Moses' two sons ... vv. 5, 6. They arrived while Moses and the people were camped at Mount Sinai.

"Moses went out to meet his father-in-law and greeted him warmly; they asked about each other's health and then went into Moses' tent to talk further. Moses related ... all that had been happening and what the Lord had done ... and all the problems there had been along the way, and how the Lord had delivered his people from all of them.

"Jethro was very happy about everything the Lord had done for Israel and about him bringing them out of Egypt. Bless the Lord, Jethro said, for he has saved you ... I know now that the Lord is greater than any other god because he delivered his people from the proud and cruel Egyptians."

EXODUS 18:1–10

IT WAS NOT through a Christian teacher that I received one of the most revolutionary revelations about God in the whole course of my life. It was through a poor Moslem woman and then through a young orthodox Jew that they were given to me, just as Moses received much-needed light through his father-in law, Jethro, the priest of a non-Israelite tribe and faith.

One winter I was staying in a Moslem town in the Jordan valley, living in rented rooms with a young Arab Christian nurse and visiting with her in the neighboring villages. There was no clinic or medical help of any kind in the whole of that district filled with scattered Arab villages. There were no shops and no road, just a waterlogged dirt track in winter. We were miles away from any modern amenities of any kind; we had no running water and no electricity, only sputtering candles.

One evening my Arab nurse friend came to me in a troubled state. She said that a poor Moslem woman whom she had been trying to help was at the point of death and ought to be driven at once to the Nazareth Mission Hospital many miles away. But we were in a terrorist-infested area with armed infiltrators coming over the frontier from Jordan nearly every night with explosives and ammunition. So strict curfew was imposed every evening. Anyone seen moving outside would be looked upon as up to some evil purpose, and the police would shoot at them or terrorists would snipe at them and plunder whatever they had in their possession.

The nurse begged me to drive her and the woman to the hospital, but we could not possibly get there before nightfall, and the curfew was due to start in about half an hour. We prayed earnestly about it and decided that the Lord was calling us to go. What a drive it was! Never before had I had such an experience. We seated the woman in the back of the car with the nurse, and we set off along a bumpy, hole-riddled dirt track toward the distant Nazareth hills. Darkness fell the moment the sun set, but I dared not turn on the car lights for fear of attracting attention in that lonely wasteland. I could see practically nothing in the darkness, but the little car was filled with the presence of the loving Savior himself. Mile after mile we struggled along, and it was as though he sat beside me, tenderly encouraging and reassuring me. At last we came to the hairpin bends on the Nazareth hills, and I simply had to turn on the lights and risk being seen. So we went on ever upwards and at last came to Nazareth and up the last steep hill to the mission hospital in the dead of night.

Then as the woman was taken from the car and carried through the hospital door on a stretcher, she died. The long dangerous drive had been in vain. Her life ended before she, a poor village Moslem woman, could hear a single word about the Lord Jesus, the loving Savior, and now she would never be able to hear the gospel news.

As I lay on one of the hospital beds for the rest of that night, I turned to the Lord in an agony of sorrow and bewilderment. "Lord," I gasped, "why did you let us make that frightfully dangerous drive all in vain and risk our lives so that this poor Moslem woman might have the opportunity to hear about you and respond and be saved? Why did you not let her hear anything about you and experience your loving-kindness and help here in the mission hospital? Why has she gone to a lost eternity? Did you not love her and die for her too, just as you did for us? Yet now she can never know you nor experience your love and saving power."

Then vividly the voice of the Lord himself spoke tenderly and gently in my thoughts. "Hannah, on that long, dark, dangerous, hopeless drive, of what were you most conscious?"

And I whispered back, "Lord, I was more conscious that you were with us in the car than of anything else."

"Then, Hannah, don't you think that when that Moslem woman breathed her last breath on the hospital stretcher and her earthly consciousness ended, that the first thing she would become aware of would be me telling her that I loved her and was there with her, ready to take her home to our Father and to his eternal love? There she would be able to hear everything about me that she never had the opportunity to hear on earth and to respond with all her own heart's love."

"Lord," I whispered, "surely that ought to be the glorious fact, but it does not say so in the Bible. In fact, it says just the contrary."

"'Does not say so,'" the loving Lord echoed. "Why, whatever do you mean? I myself kept declaring all the time I was on earth, as is recorded in all the Gospels, that God so loved the world of fallen sinners that he gave everything to save it, that he is *the Savior of all men*, and that he has the keys of hell and of death, not to lock anyone into them forever but to fling the gates wide open and let them out."

So he led me to these beautiful verses in the Bible: 1 Timothy 2:3, 4, Romans 11:32, John 1:29, 1 Timothy 4:10, 1 John 2:2, John 12:32, John 4:42, 1 John 4:14, Revelation 5:13, and many others.

It was there in the Nazareth Hospital that the transforming light shone into my understanding, and I saw a more wonderful God and Savior than I had ever been able to see before—more inexpressively loving and powerful and perfectly just and good and more worthy a thousand times over to be adored and loved and thanked and blessed.

From that night on I have never doubted the glorious fact that he is indeed "the Savior of all men" *and women*. Not a single soul is lost forever! The loving Savior gets a one hundred percent victory and the devil gets none. Not one single soul will be lost, but God pledges that every last one of us will be not only fully restored but also able to love and adore and worship him to a far greater degree than would ever have been possible if we had not fallen into sin and experienced his forgiving love. For as the Savior himself said, "He that is forgiven much, loveth much."

The next morning, because Moslem law forbids that any Moslem body be buried near Christian infidels, it was my duty to drive the body of the woman back to her native village. There her husband and friends came with a stretcher and spades and dug a hole in the ground and took the body from the car and, just as it was, laid it in the ground and buried it.

Then with newborn rapture in my heart I prepared to continue spreading the good news of God's eternal triumphant love and power to save. But for a long time I dared not tell my Christian friends and fellow workers about the new transforming light that had been poured into my soul, for they believed just the opposite—that death is the end of the opportunity to hear and respond and be saved. But surely that is not good news, but the very worst news possible! It makes the devil stronger than God and gives him a greater victory than the Savior's! But for me, all eternity now shone bright with a dazzling glory, for every single soul is to be rescued and saved; indeed each one is undergoing that blessed process now and finally will be able to cooperate with our triumphant Father God in creating nothing but the highest possible good.

But one last huge question remained in my mind and thoughts. If this glorious illumination is true, why does the Bible speak so much about *hell* and describe it over and over again as being everlasting punishment?

Our loving Father in heaven had another overwhelmingly unexpected and glorious answer to that question too. And I received it as it were through Jethro once again, namely another non-Christian believer and worshiper of God.

Before starting the work of distributing free Bibles and New Testaments around the country, in order to become more fluent in the Hebrew language I had gone to stay as a paying guest in the home of a young orthodox Jewish couple. It might seem unexpected that strictly practicing Jews would be willing to receive a woman Christian missionary into their home, even as a paying boarder. But the young wife had recently given birth to their first child and now was beginning to wean it from breast-feeding to a milk diet. The tiny creature needed warm drinks every few hours, and the couple were so strictly orthodox that they did not feel it right to turn on either the electric light or the cooker after the ram's horn was blown on the eve of the Sabbath until the end of the next day. That meant that they were obliged to leave the light and cooker turned on all through the Sabbath night and day, and electricity at that period was fantastically expensive. When I asked if they would accept a paying boarder for a few weeks, they were glad to receive me, for I could act as what is called in Yiddish "a Shabbath goi," that is, a non-Jew who could turn the light and the cooker on and off when necessary so that the baby's milk could be heated. They must not ask me to do this, but I was to watch the times carefully on other days when the mother warmed the milk. As soon as twilight fell on Friday evening I was to turn on the necessary lights and to be *very* sure to turn them off again without being asked to do so when everyone went to bed. Besides that, they were as eager to learn English and practice speaking it with someone as I was to learn Hebrew, for English was the business language of the mandatory government, and all the best-paying salaries went to those who could both speak and write it.

So the agreement was made, and I joined the little family and passed a happy and intensely interesting five or six weeks with them. It was a great help to be living in a home where fluent Hebrew was spoken all the time. We devised a system whereby we alternately carried on conversations in Hebrew and English in a most interesting fashion. We had long talks together, especially at mealtimes and in the evenings after their day's work was over, and we often took the opportunity to talk about our different religious views.

One evening the young man asked me in halting English why I had taken upon myself the debasing employment of becoming a missionary, one of the most uncomplimentary names an orthodox Jew can apply to any human being (except one still worse describing a convert from Judaism to Christianity). I then explained in my halting Hebrew that I wanted to be able to talk about the greatest Jew who ever lived, Jesus of Nazareth, and how we can all be saved and helped to turn from sin by believing on him and obeying the things he taught.

Then the young man said, "And what if people do not believe on him but sincerely consider him to be a liar and blasphemer?"

I was filled with great distress and plainly showed it. Then I painfully explained that I believed that if people who heard about him refused to accept him as their Savior, they were preparing terrible sorrow and suffering for themselves which would last forever.

The young man looked at me for a moment in silence and then said with the most solemn earnestness, "Miss Hurnard, I, as a devout and earnest Jew, could never believe in, trust, worship, or long to obey the commandments of a God who would permit an endless hell and slavery to evil. I cannot accept a God who chooses to go on bringing untold multitudes of souls into existence whom he cannot prevent from continuing to go on sinning and blindly rejecting him all their life long, whom he then actually damns to endless punishment and suffering because he himself cannot win them to love and long to worship him and keep his laws.

"That seems to me to be a diabolical conception of the Most High Almighty God. I myself was privileged to be born into an orthodox Jewish family and to learn from childhood about the one true God and how to reverence and serve him as he desires. You, however, were born into a Gentile family ignorant of the one true God and therefore are in spiritual blindness and darkness. But I can never suppose for a moment that because of that fact, you are lost eternally and that God our Creator rejects you and cares for me only. No! Sometime, if you do not seek to be received into the community of God's chosen people in this life-

time, you will be allowed to return to another life here on earth
and be born into a Jewish family and so learn to believe in the
One True God and to reverence and serve him as he desires all
souls to do. That is the only truly just and righteous God in
whom I can believe, or even desire to do so."

Well! There it was! What a message to be given to a Christian
missionary by a Jethro-like worshiper of another religion! I was
stunned by the shock of it, by the completely new shattering idea
that perhaps spirits return to earth life more than once and have
the opportunity at last to learn the real saving truth about God,
which they had not known before.

I did not dare even to consider the idea at that time but inwardly rejected it with horror and shock. But after the experience with the poor Moslem woman, those words of the young
orthodox Jew shone into my mind with astonishing new light
and power. Supposing they were true after all! Would that not
explain all the bewildering questions about why some have the
opportunity to hear the gospel and multitudes more do not? And
supposing that all the hells are here on earth, not in some far
distant bodiless state, but right here, experienced by means of
another physical body in another lifetime after the death of this
present one. How likely that suddenly seemed to be! For does
not the inspired Old Testament plainly tell us that in ancient
times human beings lived to be hundreds of years old and so
had ample time to experience the results of evil doing and spiritual blindness and to long for deliverance and light? If we have
the opportunity to learn the full truth about God and how to
become conscious of him only during one short lifetime of a
few years—at the very most one hundred, and generally far less
than that how unjust and cruel that would be.

But oh! Did not Jesus himself continually speak about this very
fact by again and again referring to the difference between "life"
and "eternal life" and the vital importance of "being born again"

somewhere, sometime and so recovering our lost consciousness of the One True God and how to love and serve him aright. "Neither can they die any more; for they are equal unto the angels; and are the children of God, being the children of the resurrection." (Luke 20:36). Surely that is a plain statement that then they will not need to return to another lifetime on earth but will have learned the glorious message that earth life is meant to teach us. That sin and selfishness can never satisfy but actually create hells of suffering here on earth, and only God himself, known and loved with the whole heart can create a real heaven of joy and perfect satisfaction.

So when in any lifetime souls become purged of all longing to continue living according to their own fallen self-will and self-centered desires, they are privileged to hear the glorious Good News of the Savior who can cleanse and completely deliver them and restore their lost God-consciousness and delight in doing his will. The purpose of earth life and of what is called the experience of hell and death and the grave, ends and they receive restored eternal life and will not need to die any more.

The Apostle Paul explains this to the non-Jewish Gentile believers. He told them that without knowledge of the Lord Jesus and the saving truth that he brought, earthly mortal life is like being buried in a grave Sheol or hell in a state of spiritual death and loss of God-consciousness. And meeting with Jesus the Savior is like waking from that spiritual death and leaving the temporary gravelike mortal life and experiencing resurrection to eternal life, to "die no more."

So in Ephesians 5.14 we read, "Awake thou that sleepest and rise from the dead and Christ shall give thee life."

This is not the teaching of reincarnationists who believe that spirits keep returning to mortal bodies over and over again and growing more pure and divine each time. Jesus taught differently. He said that as soon as we have the opportunity to meet and respond to him, we enter upon eternal life and will not need to return to another lifetime and die once again. There may well be a difference in belief and opinion as to whether all the hells are here on earth; or are some mythical fire and brimstone experience in some other realm altogether. But how awesome and dreadful is the thought that if we who have the privilege of hearing the gospel news reject it, we condemn ourselves to return to the sort of hellish life we read and hear about in the newspapers and see continually depicted on the television screen! And how glorious and wonderful to know that if we respond to the light and are born again to our lost God-consciousness, when these present mortal bodies die we shall go at once to our blessed home in the heavenly world and "die no more"! In the Hebrew language, the only thing that is endless is God, Himself: "The Endless One." Evil and hell are not endless.

A flood of new glorious light shone into my understanding as this truth so long-lost to Christians but well attested to in the Bible, was returned to me through that faithful young orthodox Jew. Thank God indeed for the wonderful way in which step by step he loves to guide us into more and more truth and will do so until the full truth becomes visible to us!

15

The Workers Who Helped Moses

Moses' father-in-law ... said, "Why are you trying to do all this alone? ... This job is too heavy a burden for you to handle all by yourself. ... Find some capable, godly, honest men ... and appoint them as judges. ... It will be easier for you because you will share the burden with them, ... and if the Lord agrees you will be able to endure the pressures and there will be peace and harmony in the camp."

EXODUS 18:14–21, 23

DURING THOSE eleven years of heavy work and danger, the loving Lord gave me wonderful friends and helpers to share the load and make it possible to reach every place. What a debt of gratitude I owe to them, and what wonderfully important lessons we learned together and, by God's grace, through each other! We were all so utterly different in temperament, upbringing, training, nationality, and language; we had various suggestions to make and methods to try out; and, thank God, we had such diverse experience and understanding of the many nationalities and outlooks of the people to whom we sought to witness. The Jewish immigrants came from many nations, and they spoke about sixty languages when they first arrived and while learning the Hebrew language. But all our needs were wonderfully met, and health and protection were granted to us.

Then at last, when every place in the country had been visited, some of them several times, as well as many villages and towns in Lebanon, the Hauran, and Transjordan, we were able to rest from the work, as all cars were ordered off the roads. We thanked the Lord with adoring gratitude for eleven years of carrying the Scriptures all over the Holy Land. It was the first time since the destruction of Jerusalem in A.D. 70 and the dispersion of the Jewish nation all over the then known world that it had been possible to give a witness to the Lord Jesus in every place in the country. The Roman conquerors forcibly prohibited it, as did the later Moslem Turkish regime. Not until General Allenby entered Jerusalem in 1918 and the British mandatory rule was established was this prohibition removed. Then the witness became possible, even during the years of terrorism until it ended in 1947. By then every place had been reached.

For eight years it had not been possible for me to travel home to England. World War Two had broken out in 1939, and travel became impossible. But just before that happened my father had been able to send me a second car so that we had three at our disposal for the work. How wonderful that was, as God's timing always is perfect!

When the last place had been reached and the three cars taken off the roads, I went thankfully to rest for a time in Jerusalem, where some of my closest friends and fellow workers belonging to various missions lived.

It was there in Jerusalem in 1947 that unexpectedly another test awaited us, the greatest of all to that point. A series of terrorist uprisings had taken place during which British people were being taken captive and held for ransom, including a judge sitting in a court in full session. When that happened the mandatory government felt obliged to pass an edict stating that within three days all British women and children in the country must be evacuated to safety, for the terrorists were threatening to take a number of them and hold them as hostages in order to force the government to accede to their demands and to give up the mandate. So only the British military forces were to remain in the land, to quell the rampant armed terrorism in both the Jewish and Arab portions of the country.

Wives were suddenly parted from their husbands in the armed forces, who were left to deal with the frightfully dangerous situation now at boiling point. Perhaps some of the women would never see their husbands again. All the missionaries also had to pack suddenly and leave in three days' time and join the crowd of women and children in an air shuttle service from Palestine to Egypt. There we would spend some time in the Maadi Military Camp until we could safely cross the Mediterranean and be taken home to England.

This whole tragic affair was labeled "Operation Polly" by the government, but at once almost everyone involved in it changed the name to "Operation Folly." I must bear grateful witness to the fact that the whole scheme was carried out in a praiseworthy and considerate manner with the least possible hardship and difficulty. But certainly for the vast majority of sorrowful women and bewildered and frightened children, it was a very sad time.

I met my best friend and companion in the work at the airport, where we were all marshalled in groups ready for the flight to Egypt. It was an unforgettable and indescribable experience, and the fact that it began with an air shuttle service added to my personal turmoil. I still had dreadful claustrophobic feelings and a horror of heights, and I had determined that I would never travel by air. Yet here I was, about to be shut in a small place with no possible means of getting out, to be lifted up thousands of feet in the air. Oh, what would happen to me? But the presence of the Lord was wonderfully real and comforting as flight time approached.

With a crowd of weeping women and frightened children, I ascended a stepladder to a trap door in the floor of a crazy-looking, old-fashioned bomber airplane. It was utterly unlike modern planes and their interior arrangements. Long, hard seats ran from end to end of the bomber, not arranged in rows but fixed to the two sides of the plane, with no cushions or any kind of comfort. On these we perched, our legs dangling. The floor door was slammed, a siren wailed, and we took off.

And there in that ancient, comfortless, sorrow-filled old bomber, a most beautiful thing happened to me. I sat with my back to the window, afraid of being overcome by the height. Then as soon as we were in the air, the wonder began. I heard what seemed to be exquisite heavenly harmonies, as though beautiful celestial choirs were playing on harps and violins, and deep organ symphonies filled the air all around the plane. I had never heard anything like it before, and I sat entranced while healing music filled my heart and soul with ecstasy. All heaven seemed to be singing consolation in tender oneness and sympathy with that crowd of heartbroken women and frightened children. But, strangely, no one else seemed to hear it.

I sat there awed, wondering why no one had ever hinted that flying in the air meant passing through realms of heavenly music, and why did no one else seem to be conscious of it? What did it mean? Oh! I could never dread flying in an airplane again!

It was a short flight, and soon the old bomber descended to the earth and pulled to a stop. We filed out through the floor, down the rickety old steps. We were greeted by a dignitary in military uniform and then were driven in motorcade to Maadi Camp and appointed to our dormitories. There we stayed until we could be shipped home to England by boat. I never heard the heavenly music again on any other flight. But that evacuation flight proved to be a wonderful preparation for the ministry to which the Lord was just about to call me, for I had lost all my fear of flying and it never returned.

So I returned home to my loving father and the kind wife he had married. I was able to rest day by day in the beautiful garden I loved so much and to rejoice in communion with the Lord and ask to be shown his will for my future life and witness. I had many questions: Why I had been called away so unexpectedly from the mission field? Why had the evacuation happened? What were his new plans? Was I to return to Palestine, or was the missionary service from 1932 to 1947 now ended? If so, where did God want me to serve him next?

After four months of rest and enjoying home life again, all these questions were answered in the most unexpected way. I was allowed the great joy of having my most beloved missionary friend come and stay with us for a visit. She, of course, with all the other British missionaries had been evacuated. We spent lovely hours together in fellowship with the Lord, remembering and praying for the sorrowful, terrorist-ridden, suffering land from which we had been forcibly but kindly and protectingly removed.

One day while my friend was still with me, I received a news sheet from the Church Mission to the Jews, containing their latest requests for prayer and reporting on the work in Palestine. The mission was seeking special prayer support for the medical staff who had been allowed to remain in the Jerusalem Mission Hospital, which was in the part of the city where most of the population was Jewish, though a number of the nurses were Arabic. Now the tension between Jews and Arabs was so great that it was not safe for any Arab nurses to remain in the Jewish area, and they and the Arab housekeeper would have to leave the hospital as soon as a substitute housekeeper could be found. Jewish nurses were not available, nor a Jewish housekeeper, because the religious Jews were so incensed against the British and the

Christian hospital. So earnest prayer was asked that a suitable housekeeper could be found to take the place of the Arab one and make it possible for the small British staff to carry on at least part of their work.

I read the mission news sheet to my friend so that we could immediately join in praying that the need would be met. I said in a melancholy voice, "Whoever volunteers for that work will have a frightfully difficult task to fulfill and will certainly need special prayer support and grace to cope with such a dangerous situation. Terrorists are already threatening to destroy any Jewish or Hebrew Christian nurses who believe in the Lord Jesus, because the orthodox Jews look upon them as being traitors and paid employees of the hated mandatory government." Then I prayed, "Oh dear Lord, please provide the hospital housekeeper they need so much; and oh Lord Jesus, we feel so terribly sorry for her whoever she turns out to be, and give her the special grace that she will so greatly need."

The next day's mail contained a letter addressed to me from the Church Mission to the Jews. On opening it I read with horror and amazement that the committee members were asking me if I would return to Jerusalem and become the much-needed hospital housekeeper. They were almost certain that they could gain the necessary government permission for me to do so, because the hospital work was greatly needed in those times of so much fighting and terrorism.

The tremendous shock caused by the absurdity of this suggestion was overwhelming. Me, a housekeeper for a hospital? When I was an unmarried evangelist and knew absolutely nothing about housekeeping even for myself, much less for a whole hospital! I would not be able to tell anyone what to do or what to buy in the way of food provisions. The only thing I could cook was a piece of toast. How did such a crazy idea ever enter their heads?

The letter went on to say that the real need was for someone who could speak both Hebrew and Arabic and had experience dealing with both Jews and Arabs and sympathizing with their totally different points of view. Someone on the Jerusalem staff had suggested my name as being almost the only person they knew who had been led to work among both groups. For all the Christian missions worked exclusively among either Arabs or Jews, but not both.

"Well!" I exclaimed, when I had read the astounding letter to my friend. "I shall of course write at once and tell them that it is quite impossible, for I know absolutely nothing about housework of any kind, or cooking either."

My friend, who knew me well indeed, for we had lived together for two or three years, could not help agreeing that I did seem to be a most unsuitable person for the job. But then she added that only yesterday we had both prayed that someone would receive a call to do it, and that I myself had added earnestly, "And Lord Jesus, please give that person special enabling grace for what looks like such an overwhelmingly difficult and unattractive position."

She was right. So all I could pray now was, "Lord, do you really want me to answer this letter and tell them that I am willing to volunteer?"

Then the Lord said, "Yes. Answer the letter at once. Tell them with absolute honesty that you know nothing about housework or cooking and you were never involved in learning it. Since your Bible school days you have never shared in community life but have lived and worked with only one or two other people. And then be joyfully willing to let me show you my will and purpose through whatever reply you receive."

So I wrote and posted the letter, and almost at once received an answer from the mission committee saying that they gladly accepted my offer. All the hospital staff had been well trained by the present housekeeper who now had to leave, and I would need to be there only to encourage and help the staff, to listen to their requests, and to go to the shops and buy what they told me was needed, for none of them was allowed to drive about in a car and do the shopping. But my own little car, with special license and permission for me to use it, had been left parked on the hospital compound when I was evacuated to England and had nowhere else to leave it. They could get permission for me to return almost at once and begged me to be ready to do so.

Even my dear father was dubious about the wisdom of responding to this new call. But the Lord gave great peace and assurance that I was right to do so, though consternation and alarm filled my heart. But also I felt great joy in the thought of being allowed to return to the land where I had been working with him for so long. I knew by then that it is always safe to put one's hand in the hand of the loving Lord, and to go with Him up to even the most terrifying looking scarecrow with full assurance that all the best and richest blessings will be waiting close beside the most terrifying situations. So in a very short time, that same year of the evacuation in 1947, there was I, one solitary British woman, being allowed to fly back to Palestine.

My father and stepmother had bade me a most loving farewell and prayed for me to receive God's special enabling grace to meet the new challenge. It was the last time I saw my father. He went to be with the Lord before my next visit to England. Thus in an extraordinary way I was allowed to have that truly blessed farewell visit with him. And I learned from his own lips that the fact that for all those years he had a daughter living and witnessing in the very land where the Lord Jesus had lived and worked, and that she had been able to share in placing the gospel news in every place in the country, had been the greatest privilege and joy he had ever experienced.

Yes, like the psalmist, rejoicingly I can exclaim, "This is the Lord's doing, and it is marvelous in our eyes!"

And I have learned and proved the truth of this glorious spiritual lesson that *everything voluntarily laid down into death at the Lord's command* will be raised again in some more glorious form. Bless the Lord, O my soul, and let us exalt his name together!

16

The Mountain Smoked

The Israelis arrived in the Sinai Peninsula ... and set up camp there. Moses climbed the rugged mountain to meet God, and from somewhere in the mountain God called to him. ... "I am going to come to you in the form of a thick cloud: Go down now and see that the people are ready for my visit. Sanctify them". "... On the morning of the third day there was a terrific thunder and lightening storm and a huge cloud came down upon the mountain, and there was a long, loud blast ... and all the people trembled. Moses led them out from the camp to meet God. All Mount Sinai was covered with smoke, because Jehovah descended upon it in the form of fire; the smoke billowed into the sky as from a furnace and the whole mountain shook with a violent earthquake". ... So the Lord came down upon the top of Mount Sinai and called Moses up to the top of the mountain, and Moses ascended to God.

EXODUS 19:1–20

THE RETIRING HOUSEKEEPER remained at the hospital for two or three weeks after I arrived. She showed me around and explained what my duties would be—overseeing the work of the well-trained domestic staff and ordering all the necessary food supplies.

One unexpected task she impressed upon me as being very important. The patients in the hospital were all poor Palestinian Jews and Arabs who could not afford to go to any of the other hospitals; neither could they buy anything in the shops, for prices were then exhorbitantly high and most things had to be bought in the "black market," which only the rich could afford to do. So they were greatly tempted to smuggle items of hospital linen such as towels, pillow slips, vests, nightgowns, and many other small items. It was imperative to search them all before they left, or the hospital would soon be denuded of a vast quantity of linen and other equipment, which could be replaced only by paying black market prices for it and, indeed, probably buying back much of the same linen patients would have sold there.

So it was my duty to put my hand down the back and front of each departing patient, including the little children, and feel beneath their ragged garments and recover whatever I could. What an assortment of unexpected items I always discovered! The inspection was carried on in another room where the other patients could not see what was happening. I would pull out a towel from under the back part of the garment and a pillow slip from the front and some face cloths from the dress of a small child, and always the patients would look at me with big wondering eyes as though I were a magician or conjuror producing objects from nowhere. No word of scolding was ever uttered, and though a great deal of hospital equipment was thus fortunately retrieved, it did seem sad to think of the poor patients' disappointment at having to return to their poverty-stricken homes bereft of such precious treasures.

Soon after I arrived back in Jerusalem, it became clear why the Lord had opened the way for me to return. I still had my little car and permission to buy gasoline, and I spent a great deal of time taking not only the Arab housekeeper to her home in another town in Palestine, but also, one by one, the other Arab helpers too. It was not at all an easy or safe task, for snipers were on the watch to attack the few cars passing from one area to another. But in the end it was safely accomplished, and no Arabs were left in the hospital in the Jewish part of the city. And just in time! For soon afterwards partition was carried out, and one-half of Palestine became Arab territory and one-half Jewish, and there was absolutely no intercourse between them. Then, just a little later, Great Britain declared its intention of laying down the mandate and leaving the Jews and Arabs to confront one another alone, waging war on each other and maintaining by armed force the two partitions in the land.

It became clear that the hospital must be closed and the British staff leave the country before war broke out. Just two members of the Church Mission to Jews remained behind, the Reverend Ronald Adeney, the minister, and dear Ruth Clarke, the much-loved principal of the mission school for girls—and me! It was my work to drive back and forth through the British military zone taking the workers to the mission hostel in the Arab area, from where they were to be driven by armed escort to the airport and flown home to England. Also I took the opportunity to buy food supplies for the three of us who were to remain behind and for a handful of missionaries from other nations who also elected to stay in Jewish Jerusalem. It was quite clear that as soon as the British military left, Jewish Jerusalem would be in a state of complete siege, for it was situated in the Arab area and quite a distance from the Jewish half of the country.

So in the summer of 1948, Jewish Jerusalem was left in a state of siege, surrounded by Arab forces from neighboring Arab counties as well as the Palestinians. No intercourse was possible with any part of the Jewish area in Palestine. Armies, land mines, and bombshells made all movement out of the Jewish area impossible. The mission hospital was handed over to the Jews, because their own huge hospital was outside the Jewish area among the Arabs and was quickly seized by them. But Ronald Adeney, Ruth Clarke, and I were allowed to remain in a little building on the hospital grounds throughout the siege.

So there we were in Jewish Jerusalem with no hospital for me to supervise. Our small house had its own well and pump so that we did not have to join the queues going to obtain their water ration under constant shell firing and sniping. That was indeed a wonderful blessing, for all the water pipelines were cut off by the Arabs so that no water could enter our part of the city. That is why Jewish forces immediately rushed in and occupied all the houses and buildings left empty by the evacuating British, United States, and German citizens in the areas of the new city. Most of those empty premises had their own wells, and these were immediately guarded by the Jewish forces, who then strictly rationed the pumped water to the besieged inhabitants, trusting that the wells would not run dry before the rainy season began and replenished them.

When the British forces left the country, the isolation of Jewish Jerusalem was indeed complete. Even during the months after partition, while the British were still in authority, it had become impossible to pass from the Jewish half of Jerusalem to the Arab half and vice versa unless one had a permit to go through the British military zone, which I had. In order to continue shopping in the main street, where the Jewish and Arab sections met and were guarded by armed soldiers belonging to both groups, it would have been necessary to get on an airplane in the Jewish area (and there were none), fly over the sea to the Island of Cyprus, change planes, fly back to the mainland over Lebanon and Syria and then Jordan; land in the Israeli part of the Jordan valley, and make the long drive up the mountains to Jerusalem and so back to the main shopping center just two minutes' walk from one's starting point. Oh, the fantastic craziness of it!

The verses at the beginning of this chapter describe in a most vivid way a picture of conditions as they then existed for everyone who remained in the Jewish area of Jerusalem throughout the 1948 siege. "The Lord said, 'I am going to come to you in the form of a thick cloud'" (Exod. 19:9). "There was a terrible thunder and lightening storm" (v. 16). For shells and bombs fell on the city and there were clouds of smoke and flashing flames "and all the people trembled." All Mount Sion (not Mount Sinai) and the mountain on which Jerusalem is built were "covered with smoke billowing into the sky as from a furnace and the whole mountain shook" with the bursting shells, and it seemed as though violent earthquakes were taking place.

Every day many people were killed by the explosions, blown to pieces, one of them at the gate of the little house in which Ronald, Ruth, and I were living. All the dead were taken to our hospital compound or to the Roman Catholic hospital a little further along the street, and to one or two small Jewish ones. Every day the bodies lay there surrounded by eastern Jewish women wailing their loved ones. One of the horrors of the siege was that there were no cemetaries nor burial places in the be-sieged part of the city, and the bodies had to be placed in the hospital grounds until nightfall. Then, under cover of darkness, they were secretly taken away and piled up on one another in some caves that, fortunately, were just within the besieged area, though on the very outskirts of it. After the siege ended they were taken away and given a mass burial.

Night after night as the sirens screamed and the shells explod-ed, Ruth and I lay on mattresses in the basement of the little house on the hospital compound. Over and over again we were comforted by the words of Psalm 91, as the mountain quaked and a great cloud covered the whole city: "I will say of the Lord, he is my refuge . . . In Him will I trust." Though a thousand shells shall fall at thy side and ten thousand explosions take place the Lord will be our protector and no evil shall befall us. "For he shall give his angels to keep us and guard us in all our ways. There shall no evil come nigh our dwelling place." And so it was!

17

The Thick Darkness
Where God Was

*All the people saw the thunderings, and the lightenings, . . . and
the mountain smoking. . . . And Moses said unto the people, Fear
not: for God is come to prove you, and that his fear may be
before your eyes, that ye sin not. And the people stood afar off,
and Moses drew near unto the thick darkness where God was.*

EXODUS 20:18–21 KJV

DURING THE SIEGE the dear Lord gave me a completely
unexpected and comforting pleasure. A small terrier dog had been
left tied to a garden gate in one of the areas from which everyone
had been evacuated in 1947. Its owners had evidently been unable
to take it with them and hoped someone might find it and take
compassion on it. A woman found it and asked me if I would take
care of the dog and I agreed. I called the little creature Charlie, and
he instantly became my devoted companion and friend and could
not bear to let me out of his sight. In all my adventurous journeys
conveying the hospital staff to their different zones, he went with
me in the car, and we became inseparable.

At nighttime when shells came crashing down I let him lie on
the mattress at my feet, but that did not satisfy him. As soon as
an explosion or sound of shooting occurred, he would creep a
little further up the mattress, until at last he could snuggle right
up close to me and I would put my arm around him. Then he
would give one huge sigh of relief and contentment, relax, and

fall fast asleep and never stir or tremble again when future crashes occurred. He and I seemed to become able to talk to each other in a wonderful way so that he could understand me and I him. So once I asked him as he snuggled up close beside me, "Charlie, what makes you so peaceful and unafraid when I put my arm around you? You know that if a shell did crash down on us I could do nothing to save you."

"Oh, I know that all right," he seemed to say quite happily. "But the shining people who are always around about you, talking to you and looking after you, would take you away at once to the beautiful place where they live. I think that if I am snuggled right up close against you and your arm is around me, that they will think that I am a part of you and they will take me too. So I won't be left all alone again as I was before."

Dear, loving little Charlie. What a precious God-given gift and comfort you were to me again and again all through the siege! Often after you told me that I would find myself saying to our heavenly Father, "Please make me as happily unafraid as this dear little dog. Keep me abiding in your presence, held fast in your loving arms and so safely protected from fear and evil of any kind." Thank God that he can speak to us and teach us through everything that he has created and remind us of his loving-kindness.

Perhaps one of the most unexpected and precious experiences during that time of being "in the thick darkness where God was" with me all the time, was the challenge to remind myself every morning that *"this is the day that the Lord hath made; I will rejoice and be glad in it"* (Ps. 118:24). And then I discovered that in a strange and beautiful way amid all the dangers and constant awareness that death might come at any time, there was heightened in me to an amazing degree the power to appreciate all the beauties of nature and to enjoy them in a way I had never before been able to do—the green trees, the glorious hibiscus flowers, the blue delphiniums in the hospital flower beds, the fresh cool air which drove away the awful stench when the east wind blew into the caves where all the dead bodies were laid, the songs of the birds. Yes, and the times when Ruth, Ronald, and I sang the old Moody and Sankey hymns together as I pedaled away on the hospital harmonium.

But best of all were the flocks of pigeons shining white in the sunset, as each evening they rose from both Jewish and Arab areas in the city and mingled happily in the sky as though there were no barriers of any kind. They knew no closed Mandelbaum Gate where the two areas met, no hideous land mines, and no armed forces of hatred and violence confronting each other down on the earth below. Oh you wonderful, dear birds so beautifully symbolizing peace and goodwill. How lovely and reassuring your evening messages were as you soared over the war-wracked city and demonstrated the beauty of friendship and unity without barriers of any kind! Evening by evening you taught me to "worship in the beauty of holiness" and to forgive in tender love.

I think that perhaps the most challenging and illuminating lesson of all was what I learned in the hospital garden, where hour after hour each day the eastern Jewish women sat on the ground weeping over their dead loved ones. Over and over again they uttered one heartbreaking cry: *Ouai, ouai!* One day as I was thinking compassionately of their grief I remembered how the Lord of Love himself had wept here in this same city, and I got out my little Greek Testament in order to read the account of it. "And when he was come near, he beheld the city, and wept over it, saying, 'If thou hadst known, even thou ... the things which belong unto thy peace! but now they are hid from thine eyes. For the days shall come upon thee, that thine enemies shall cast a trench about thee, and compass [besiege] thee round, ... and shall lay thee even with the ground and thy children within thee '" (Luke 19:41–44 KJV).

As I read those verses it seemed to me that I heard him using the very same word of heartbroken sorrow and lamentation, *ouai, ouai.* And then I turned to Matthew 23:37, 38 KJV: "O Jerusalem, Jerusalem, thou that killest the prophets, and stonest them which are sent unto thee, how often would I have gathered thy children together, even as a hen gathereth her chickens under her wings, and ye would not! Behold, your house is left unto you desolate."

Once again the wailing cry, *ouai, ouai,* seemed to sound in my ears. Then I looked at the pages in the Greek Testament, and there it was in Matthew 23, repeated eight times in verses 13, 14, 15, 16, 23, 25, 27, and 29. Only each time this heartbroken, wailing cry of "alas, alas" (translated into English as "woe unto you") was addressed by the Lord Jesus to the scribes and Pharisees who were rejecting his message of love and salvation.

I had always heard those words to the scribes and Pharisees spoken as though Jesus was severely, even fiercely, rebuking them and pronouncing woe upon them. But when I realized that the word he used each time was in Greek exactly the same word as in Hebrew and Arabic and had the same meaning of "alas, alas," uttered with heartbroken sorrow and anguish, everything he said to them was completely transformed in my understanding. He was wailing over them just as the women were wailing over their dead loved ones in the hospital garden. He was not scolding, threatening, or pronouncing doom on them, but his heart was breaking with anguish over what they were doing to themselves and their loved ones. Alas, alas, they were condemning themselves to suffer appalling agonies and dangers. If only they would listen to him he would show them the true way of escape. But, alas, alas, oh woeful, heartbreaking sorrow, they would not do so.

What an astounding difference the tone of our voices can make, and what a different meaning it can give to the things we say! Now every time I read the words "woe to you hypocrites" in that chapter 23 I hear the wailing cry of the Lord himself: alas, if only you understood what agonies and sorrow your hypocrisy is going to bring upon you and your children and loved ones too.

It was there in the hospital garden during the siege of Jerusalem that the loving "Savior of all men" (1 Tim. 4:10) was revealed to me in a completely new light. He demonstrated himself the heart of our loving heavenly Father which is full of tender compassion and mercy, without condemnation and denunciation. He teaches us, therefore, never to condemn or denounce others who are following even terribly wrong ways. He bids us to grieve over them and to pray that they may be helped and rescued—to remember that those who sin most, because they have had more light than others and have rejected it, need more love and not less, more compassionate forgiveness and not hardness of heart.

This marvelous, tender lesson returns to me often when I am tempted to despise and condemn others I see doing all sorts of wrong, cruel, and unjust things. I am not to pass judgment on them but to pray compassionately for their rescue and deliverance, as well as for those whom they are wronging. *Ouai, ouai!* Alas, alas, if you only knew and understood the horror of what you are doing! Yes, the heartbreaking wails of the sorrowing women over their dead loved ones were used to teach me one of the greatest insights in my life.

God gave me another wonderful blessing during that time of the siege, for he called me to begin a writing ministry. The first two books were written at that time, just before and during the siege. And through all the years since, the gracious challenge to continue doing so has been repeated. "Write the things which thou hast seen" and heard and learned (Rev. 1:19). Share them with others. Remember, light shared brings more light, but light rejected and unshared brings darkness. So that is how the writing ministry began.

18

On the Mount with God

See, I am sending an Angel before you to lead you safely to the land I have prepared for you. Reverence him and obey all his instructions: do not rebel against him ... If you are careful to obey him, following all my instructions, then I will be an enemy to all your enemies [your temptations] ... and I will take away sickness from among you.

The Lord said to Moses, "Come up to me into the mountain and remain until I give you the laws and commandments ... so that you can teach the people from them. ... Then Moses went up the mountain and disappeared into the cloud at the top, and the glory of the Lord rested upon Mount Sinai ... And Moses disappeared into the cloud-covered mountain top."

EXODUS 23:20–25, 24:12, 15–18.

THE WEEKS PASSED by and then, by the help of the United Nations, a truce was established between the warring Jews and Arabs in Palestine, and the Jewish part of the country was called the State of Israel. It was an uneasy truce, and fighting broke out constantly along the borders of the two territories, but convoys of food were at last able to reach the Jewish half of Jerusalem, and the first mail in months also arrived.

In the first letter I received came the news that my father had passed on from this earth life and that I would never meet and enjoy being physically present with him again. My stepmother urged me to return to England as soon as possible because there were certain things that my father in his will had appointed me to do for him.

It was another almost overwhelming shock, but strangely and beautifully the verses in Exodus 20:21, 24 describe the situation. "Moses entered into the deep darkness where God was . . . And the Lord told Moses, 'Build altars where I tell you to.'" These are the altars of loving surrender to God's will and acceptance of all that he permits. The tender voice of the Savior and faithful Companion said at once, "Fear not. This new test is to see whether you have really been learning the lessons that I have been teaching you during the siege. So now come, draw nearer to me in this seeming thick darkness, for there is much more of my grace and love to discover."

Travel so soon after the siege ended was difficult and dangerous indeed, but it did become possible for me to leave. During our flight the plane was forced to land behind enemy Arab lines, where we were not taken prisoner, though on future occasions when planes from Israel had to land on Arab territory, that always happened. We were allowed to fly on, and we reached England safely.

My stepmother was wonderfully kind. She and my father had planned that when he passed on, the twenty-room house should become a Christian guest house where my stepmother would receive missionaries home on furlough and other Christian workers. She was happy to do this, and she had well-trained dependable helpers. She assured me that I was still to look upon it as my home and to go there whenever I visited England. She would keep my bedroom for me, and I could leave any special personal possessions there just as I had always done in the past.

When all arrangements were finished, the time came for me to return to the new State of Israel, where I expected to spend the rest of my life. Then my stepmother said to me ever so kindly and lovingly, "Hannah, I know that you will miss your father's weekly letters, and so I am going to write to you each week and keep you in touch with all that happens, just as I know your father would like me to do."

She has faithfully kept that promise ever since, from 1949 until the year of writing this book, 1985. She also welcomed me back to her home on all of my later visits to England. What a God-inspired blessing my father gave me in such a faithful, kind friend as my stepmother!

On the way back to Israel, my airplane landed briefly at Zurich in Switzerland, and two of my closest evacuated missionary friends, who were then resting in Switzerland, met me at the airport. We were overjoyed to see each other again, and they eagerly told me that they had just lately learned a most wonderful spiritual lesson quite unknown to them before. It was this: we are to go through each day *praising and thanking God for everything that happens, yes, every single thing, even those that look cruelly wrong and unjust.* When by God's grace we react to bad situations with praise and thanksgiving, we wave a magic heavenly wand over them, which transforms them and causes them to bring forth some especially beautiful and blessed form of goodness. My friends felt they had to come to the airport to tell me about this new insight, taught to them by a godly Swiss minister and teacher. They urged me to begin practicing it at once.

When I heard this I exclaimed, "How can we possibly praise and thank God even for the bad things that happen? That surely cannot be to his glory! Am I to begin praising and thanking him that my loving earthly father has just died, and I shall not see him again? And that my home is now to be a Christian guest house and not the beloved personal home with my father that it was for so many years? Am I to thank God that I am now flying back to all the perils, killings, battles, and continual war with the neighboring Arab countries? Surely it is impossible and it cannot be right to do that!"

"But it is right," they said urgently and happily, "and it does work, and transforms unpleasant things in a truly miraculous way. Try it yourself, Hannah, and prove how wonderfully it works. After all, anyone can easily thank and praise God for good and nice things, but there is holy, sacred, and transforming power in praising and thanking him for the things that we least want and feel it is impossible to accept."

It was thus at the Zurich airport that one of the most treasured spiritual gifts of truth was handed to me in 1949. By God's grace I have been practicing it ever since, and truly it does work like heavenly magic. It never fails, and my whole life has been enriched by this blessed knowledge. I cannot recommend it too highly to others to test it and so become heavenly magicians in this sorrowful, sin-wracked world, for more and more lovers of the Lord are greatly needed to demonstrate the holy power of *going through each day praising and thanking God for everything that happens.*

When I arrived back in Israel the Lord graciously opened the way for me to go to the island of Cyprus for a time of rest and relaxation after the tensions and tests of the hospital period in Jerusalem and the siege, and then the death of my dear, loving father.

I stayed at a guest house high on the slopes of Mount Olympus, alone as far as human friends were concerned, but with the loving Lord who "only doeth wondrous things!" And there, once more, I found myself being tenderly drawn into yet another completely new realm of spiritual joy, peace, and power unlike anything I had experienced before. There on Mount Olympus I sat communing with the Lord on one of the topmost pinnacles of a far-reaching range of mountains looking out over the whole island. Physically and spiritually, I saw everything from an entirely new point of view. Long, beautiful conversations with the Lord took place day by day and were written down in a little booklet entitled *The Secret of a Transformed Thought Life*. More about it in the next chapter.

19

The Glory of the Lord on the Mountaintop

The glory of the Lord on the mountaintop looked like a ... fire or raging fire. "And Moses disappeared into the cloud-covered mountain top and was there for forty days and forty nights."

EXODUS 24:17, 18

THERE ON ONE of the summits of Mount Olympus on the island of Cyprus, I found myself alone with the Lord in the most wonderful way for about thirty days and nights. And there I found myself telling him how I yearned to contact his power on a higher level than anything I had before known. Here I was, forty-five years old in 1950, seeking to love and serve him and to carry out his will for the past twenty-six years, and yet still feeling so strangely powerless to help others in the way that he had promised his followers would be able to do.

He knew that I was still tempted to be dreadfully critical of certain people and to let their behavior get on my nerves in a disgracefully unlike-Jesus way. And how I longed for power to be able to control my impulsive, ungracious way of speaking and reacting whenever I found my own plans and desires being thwarted by other people!

Then ever so gently and sympathetically my Lord talked in my thoughts and told me that he would now give me a key to victory and I was to begin experiencing a completely transformed thought life. From now on I must understand that the *Law of the Lord* ordains that everything that human beings desire, feel, and express in some way *begins in their thoughts*. And what they say to themselves and to others in their thoughts they will surely begin to express in words or actions or both. Therefore the key to a transformed life for which I longed so greatly was to allow the Lord to keep me from talking to myself and to say everything to him in thought instead. This must be my habit all the time and not just during the daily Quiet Times with him. What I now needed was *a transformed thought life* of unbroken dialogue with my beloved Lord. No more long dreary monologues with myself, telling myself just what I thought about the way in which other people were behaving.

Added to that I must develop cleansed speech habits when I talked to others. I was to learn the heavenly language of blessing—to speak, as the Lord Jesus did, only gracious things to other people, things that would bless and help them. That word *blessing*, which was the name of the heavenly language, means "to speak well and appreciatively and thankfully about everything and everyone."

Then the Lord went on to say that there were special ways in which I needed to let him check and change my speech habits.

1.　From that time on I must never criticize anyone again. The Bible word is *revile*—to call something by a bad name. Now I must bless and speak well of everything and not mention anything that was not good or capable of becoming good if I reacted to it in a good way myself. "For evil can only be overcome by good." I had become addicted to criticizing others, and like all addicts I must now "withdraw" from it and never again, without exception, criticize or point out the faults of others. I must not even pray about them, for that impressed those things still more on my consciousness and impelled me to express my criticism in either words or actions. God did not need me to draw attention to the faults in others under the guise of praying for them! So I must remember that every time I tried to pray to him about the faults of other people, he would quietly withdraw and leave me talking to myself and the four walls of the room.

2. I was never to grumble about anything again or moan or complain or express self-pity. Instead I was to go through each day praising and thanking God for everything that happened, just as I had learned should be done when my friends told me about it at the Zurich airport. Then I would be able to help in causing everything to bring forth some lovely and good thing to replace the apparently unpleasant things about which I was tempted to grumble.

3. I must never gossip about other people and their affairs or say anything about them that I would not say if they were present. Certainly I must never mention anything unpleasant that other people might say about them, because I had no means of knowing all the details and the facts of the case.

4. I must never say anything that would hurt the feelings of other people or cause them to feel that they were not appreciated or were even despised and unjustly misunderstood.

5. Also, I must never, never show off and to draw attention to the way in which the Lord seemed to be using me, thus trying to appear to be one of his favorites; I might be quite sure he had none!

6. I must never express resentment and anger about anything, but always seek to be reconciled and to accept lovingly and forgivingly anything unjust or unkind that others said or did to me.

7. I must absolutely stop arguing about things and trying to convince others that I was right and they were wrong when they differed with me on some particular matter.

8. And, last, I must never say anything that was impure and that might tempt others to have impure, unclean thoughts and desires awakened in them.

Those are the things the Lord seemed to be explaining to me there on the mountaintop, and later on I summed them up in these ten short maxims, suggested by the teaching of the Lord Jesus in his Sermon on the Mount.

1. Don't grumble. Be *thankful*.
2. Don't correct others but *mourn* and repent of one's own mistakes.
3. Don't resist. Be *meek*.
4. Don't show off. *Show hunger for what is right*.
5. Don't be unkind. Be *merciful*.
6. Don't be impure, but *pure-hearted*.
7. Don't be angry. Be *peacemakers*.
8. Don't gossip. Be *truthful*.
9. Don't criticize but *bless*.
10. Don't rebel but *hear and do*.

But there on Mount Olympus, I responded to these instructions with a question. "O Lord!" I exclaimed in spirit. "I am forty-five years old, and my habits are fixed. Is it really possible that my whole *thought life* and *speech habits* can really be changed and completely transformed by your grace and power?"

"Yes," said the Lord happily. "I will help you to do it. That is why I have brought you here. It is possible as long as you make no exceptions at any time, no matter how great the temptation. You personally must never compromise or say to yourself at any time, 'Well, in this situation surely I may, or even ought, to express criticism, condemnation, and disapproval.' You must make no exceptions or you will not remain delivered. Learn of me and seek my power, and it will be given to you."

That is how a wondrous transformation began in my life. It was like yet another new birth, being born again to consciousness on a higher level. I must admit at once that often I have slipped and fallen, but always the Lord restores me tenderly and lovingly.

Almost at once the most wonderful thing happened and I could scarcely believe it. An astounding miracle was taking place in my physical health. Within just a few weeks I discovered that my lifetime handicap of a stammering mouth was completely healed! I could talk just as easily as everyone else—unless I slipped back under sudden temptation and said something that was negative and not the kind of thing that they say in heaven. And it was a glorious blessing to discover that my own body could and did speak to me at once and remind me to repent and instantly receive cleansed lips again. It was also astounding, though I did not know it at once, that this miracle of a healed stammer happened at exactly the time when God was preparing to call me to a new ministry of speaking and preaching.

Not only did the stammer disappear and glorious liberty in speech take its place (at the age of forty-five), but also the life-long anemia disappeared. All the symptoms of chronic fatigue and exhaustion vanished and I no longer needed injections for it. I have not needed a single one to this day, thirty-six years later. Moreover, the prostrating neuralgia pains that I experienced so often in my head and rheumatic pain in my shoulders and frequent stiff neck also ended, and there was a greatly decreased tendency to develop feverish chills, though that did not disappear until some years later.

What an amazing wonder and joy all this was! I simply could not get over it; for up to that time I had never heard a hint about the connection between our thought and speech habits and our bodily health or sickness. Now I was able to begin to understand that all our "words become flesh" of some kind, manifest as health or disease, and all our actions become external events and happenings, which we experience in the world around us.

Oh, what an overwhelmingly joyous, though gradual discovery this was! And it was a blessing to realize that this Law of the Lord, when we know about it, becomes a great safeguard, delight, inspiration, and challenge. We cause ourselves to gravitate toward enriching and blessed circumstances of all kinds as long as we allow the Holy Spirit to maintain in us a transformed thought life and cleansed speech habits. Situations that at first sight may look like trials, even fiery ones, and sorrows and distresses, can by means of this Law of the Lord teach us to react with praise and thanksgiving and to practice all the heavenly maxims. That means that we ourselves create everything that we experience; we can change unpleasant things into wondrous blessings and find healing for our bodies. But there was a great deal more for me to learn about that in the future.

Looking back in memory at the glorious experience up there on Mount Olympus, it seems that the promise given to God's people in Exodus 23 was literally fulfilled. "Behold, I send an Angel before thee, to keep thee in the way, and to bring thee into the place which I have prepared. ... If thou shalt indeed obey his voice and do all that I speak ... mine angel shall go before thee ... And the Lord your God ... shall bless thy bread, and thy water; and I will *take sickness away from the midst of thee*" (vv. 20, 22, 23, 25 KJV).

That is exactly what began to happen and has continued ever since. Glory be to God!

20

Building a Sanctuary for the Lord to Dwell In

The Lord spake unto Moses, saying, Speak unto the children of Israel, that they bring me an offering: of every man that giveth it willingly . . . ye shall take my offering. And let them make me a sanctuary; that I may dwell among them.

EXODUS 25:1, 2, 8 LB

A SHORT TIME AFTER I returned to Israel, the Lord gave me another unexpected call. He told me that he wanted me to begin enlisting an army of intercessors around the world. These would pray that the thousands of Bibles and New Testaments placed as spiritual dynamite in every town and village in Palestine, and also in many places in the neighboring Arab countries, might be preserved and studied until the time came for the Holy Spirit to light the fuse and cause a mighty spiritual revival. So now I was to begin traveling from country to country telling God's people about this need and calling upon them to intercede and claim in his name that peace might, in God's good time, fill the land and make it truly a holy sanctuary for God to dwell in. (Exod. 25:8).

I was now to become like an "arrow hidden in his quiver (Isa. 49:2) and allow him to shoot me from place to place around the world and to trust him to make "my mouth like a sharp sword" through which he would be glorified. Everywhere I was to plead with his people to become an army of intercessors because before the Lord had formed me in my mother's womb he had called me for this purpose (Jer. 1:5). And now the time had come for me to fulfill this calling also.

Like all the Lord's other calls, this one seemed utterly absurd and impossible—only more so! I did not know anyone in other countries outside the British Isles and the Middle East, except one family of relatives in New Zealand. And I had no financial means by which to undertake world travel, just enough income to pay my own personal expenses and daily needs.

"Well," said the Lord, "you have that one address in New Zealand; make a beginning there. It will already take you halfway around the world, and you have just enough money to get you there, though no further. Then trust me to open up the way before you and to supply everything you need."

So, preposterous as it looked, I booked my flight and took off to New Zealand and soon found that a most wonderful thing was happening. It seemed that I was the first person to visit that country from the new State of Israel. All the British missionaries and people who had been evacuated just before the mandate ended had not been able to return to the Holy Land, and many churches and Christian communities in New Zealand (and in all the other countries to which I was later sent) were longing for someone to visit them and tell them about the siege and what was now happening. There was intense desire to learn more about how to pray for the needs and for God's purposes to be fulfilled and for the exploding of the scriptural dynamite that had been placed everywhere in the country.

I found wonderful hospitality and generosity everywhere and a great interest in the two books that I had already written about it. Then I was given the addresses of more people in Australia, Canada, and the United States, and more and more invitations came for me to go and visit those countries also. It was a joy and miracle. And I experienced absolutely no fear or dread of air travel since that amazing evacuation flight in the old bomber from Palestine to Egypt.

So I traveled from place to place in country after country, including the Pacific Islands. One special place was a visit to a leper colony and the opportunity to speak to the patients about the amazing love, grace, and tenderness of our heavenly Father. Everywhere the doors seemed wide open. What a change that was after so many years of having doors slammed in Palestine— often with spitting and cursing added! It was wonderful that my bodily health was strengthened as a result of that time with the Lord on Mount Olympus when he taught me about *transformed thoughts* and *cleansed lips* and the healing effect they have upon our physical bodies. I, who for forty-five years had been so handicapped by a stammering mouth, now reveled in many astonishing opportunities to speak for and about the One I loved most of all.

Often I remembered the year 1924, when as a cowering girl kneeling at the bedside in a little cottage near Keswick I had cried out in an agony of mind and heart, "I know what God, if he exists, is going to demand of me—my stammering mouth. He will tell me to stand up on platforms and jabber like an ape and not be able to articulate a single word. I won't do it! It would be like hell! But I'm in hell now and I don't know how to get out. Oh, I must yield my mouth!" What a wondrous heavenly harvest of joy had been hidden from that trembling, terrified girl, yet laid up for her to reap a quarter of a century later. None of us can adore and love our Lord enough!

Still other glorious privileges were offered to me besides travel and witnessing at meetings. I found time not only to rest and relax, but also to write more and more books. I sold them at meetings and so received the means to keep on printing more. Sometimes I had the opportunity to do a little reading myself.

One special book the Lord put in my hands right at the beginning of the first four years of travel was like spiritual dynamite to me. It exploded in my mind, smashing to pieces some of my spiritual ideas in the most overwhelming way. Then it replaced them with what seemed like a completely higher, fuller, and more glorious concept of the God I already loved more than I ever had before.

During one of the brief rest periods I was staying at a Christian guest house in New Zealand. At the table at which I sat at mealtimes was a quiet and, to my mind, a most ordinary and completely uninteresting young man. It seemed that he never had anything helpful to share with us, but just munched his food in silence. Then suddenly one day he did speak briefly. He remarked that he had just read a book of extracts from the writings of William Law's book on the spirit of love. It had exerted an astonishing and revolutionary influence upon him, and he felt that he could never be the same person again after reading it.

We waited to hear more but he was silent. I thought to myself, "Well, I've had enough revolutionary experiences to last me for the rest of my life. There surely can't be anything more wonderful for me to see and understand about God than I have been shown already. But I long for more power to love him and to help other people to come to know and experience his love too."

That night when I went to bed I could not sleep, and this was unusual. At last I thought I would put on the light and go to a bookshelf that held just a few books. Perhaps there would be something really dull and uninteresting to put me to sleep.

So I got out of bed and looked. Sure enough, I found an uninspiring little book in a plain black cover, with no foreword or jacket blurb. It was filled with page after page of what seemed to be fairly short quotations from some other book. As I crawled back into bed with the book I noted the title: *Extracts from the Spirit of Love,* by William Law.

"Oh," I thought, "this must be the book that dull young man talked about at the table that had revolutionized all his thoughts about God. Well, let's see what it does to me? Puts me to sleep, I hope!"

So I began reading, and—unbelievable as it seems—from the very first page I was held enthralled. I could not close the book but read extract after extract. Everything in my own mind and thoughts about God seemed to experience a revolution so glorious that I knew that I could never be quite the same person that I had been up to that time.

I do not remember the exact words written in the book, only the shining, awesome experience of light flooding into my mind. The first idea that gripped me was this: if there is one person in the world whom you do not want to love, you personally know nothing about God's love and what it is really like. For God is love and he loves all human beings equally. He sees them all as being living cells forming a single body, the body of his own beloved Son. Yes, all form one being—those who are suffering in their self-made hells as well as those who are being healed and rescued. So everything they do to each other they are really doing to themselves and to their Father God. For he is immanent and conscious in all of them, as well as being utterly transcendent.

I read on and on and saw clearly and with amazement that not only does our Creator Father determine to heal and rescue us all, as I had seen so vividly through the experience with the Moslem woman we drove to the Nazareth Hospital. I now understood that God lives and feels in us all. We live and experience things only because he continually breathes his own life and consciousness into us and shares in and feels everything that happens to us. God is transcendent, but he is also immanent in all that he creates. Therefore he says, "Inasmuch as you do anything to the least of these my human children, you are doing it to me too."

When I went down to breakfast the next morning, I looked across the table at the supposed dull young man and said to him, "I found and read the book you mentioned, written by William Law, and like you I know that I can never be exactly the same person that I was."

He looked at me quietly and said, "I understand just how you feel."

So I went out into the daily life in the world around me with a completely new attitude toward everyone I met. "You are part of me and I am part of you. I must love you, my neighboring cell in the body of humankind, as I love myself, because we are really one being in the sight of God our Father. What I do to you, I do to myself, and what you do to me, you do to yourselves." For this is the Law of the Lord, and the whole created universe is based upon it. We all form the body of God's one beloved Son. The Lord Jesus is the head of the body, and through him our Father breathes his life and consciousness into all of us and feels all that we do as being done to him.

What a sublime truth! It is inexpressible in words but shines with true life and light in spirit.

21

A Mercy Seat of Pure Gold

Make a mercy seat of pure gold. And there I will meet with thee and commune with thee.

EXODUS 25:17, 22 LB

There I will tell you my commandments. Be sure that every-thing you make follows the pattern that I am showing you here on the mountain.

EXODUS 25:22, 40 LB

THE MERCY SEAT represents the heart where either God's will or self will is enthroned. As I traveled from place to place during those four years, a longing grew in my heart to be able to share these marvelous new insights with others. But all the churches and groups from whom I was receiving invitations to visit wanted me to tell them about the work in Israel. They were communities of earnest Bible students, interested in prophecy and the signs foretelling the near return of the Lord Jesus at his second coming. They loved and steadfastly supported orthodox evangelical teachings, which did not permit them to believe that our Father God is determined to save every single soul in existence. Nor could they believe that no suffering in hell is endless or that unrepentant sinners, when they die, will not be forever cast aside by God. Much less could they listen to any teaching that God is immanent in all that he has created and feels all that they experience. If I tried to teach such ideas as those I would be considered an emmisary from Satan. I certainly could not stand up in their places of worship and begin to spread such a message as that.

However, the more I prayed and waited on the Lord, the more earnestly and clearly he told me that the time had come for me to bear witness to these things. So I asked him how I was to do this. The answer he gave me became quite clear. I was to write a letter explaining that I had received entirely new insights and interpretations of certain Scriptures as a result of witnessing for many years in the Holy Land and then passing through the siege of Jerusalem. I was to explain these interpretations in the circular letter. Then everyone who sent invitations to me to visit them and speak at meetings must receive a copy of the letter and be asked to read it and decide whether they wanted me to share those things at the meetings or not. From now on I must never speak in a church or Bible study group without honestly telling them what I believed and asking if they were willing for me to share them when I spoke, as I now believed that the Lord wished me to do.

I wrote the letter, though my heart was filled with foreboding sorrow at the thought of the results that would inevitably follow. From then on door after door was closed to me, and all invitations from evangelical groups came to an end. The invitations already issued were at once canceled. Letter after letter arrived expressing not only sorrow but strong reproach and reprobation at my determination to teach these new things. Now all my books as well as my spoken teachings must be completely rejected.

So at once I found myself alone in the United States, with every door apparently closed. I had no meetings, no gifts, no book sales, and, it seemed, no more opportunities to speak about the loving Lord and Savior who was the One I loved best and desired wholeheartedly to serve and glorify.

It was undoubtedly the saddest experience that I had ever been through. As there was no sign of any further opportunities to witness, where was I to go? What was I to do? Because I had stayed away from Israel for four years instead of only one, according to the new Israeli edict I had forfeited my right to return and live there permanently. Also, many of the most painful letters came from my own home country, England, and I knew there would be no open door there either.

After sending out the circular letter I had gone to rest and await results in a rented room in California, and there the sorrow, mental suffering, and concern about the future caused a temporary bodily illness to manifest. Those who knew me in that area began spreading a rumor that I had developed cancer (thank God there was no sign of that), and that this illness was God's clear, public condemnation of my new false teachings.

So often the darkest hour is just before the brightest dawn, and this I discovered in the most wonderful way. A door of greater opportunity than I had ever known was just about to open before me.

I began to recover from the physical trouble and was nearly restored to health after this crisis of "going outside the camp" with Christ, bearing his reproach (Heb. 13:13), when one day a completely unknown and unexpected visitor came to see me. His name was Dr. Glenn Clark, and he was visiting California at that time in connection with a fellowship of people whom the Lord had gathered together to study the things written in the inspired Scriptures and to search for greater understanding of the revelations they were meant to give. This fellowship of people seeking to understand and live according to the Kingdom of Heaven teachings given by the Lord Jesus called themselves "The Camps Farthest Out." This meant that they believed they needed to go farther on and up to a higher realm of spiritual understanding, which could be found only by going outside the camp of orthodox Christian teachings and religious ordinances.

Dr. Glenn Clark said that he had been told about the circular letter that I had written and had been shown one of the books.

God had laid it on his heart to come and see me, for the ideas
and insights that I had described in that letter and book were
very much in harmony with those accepted and witnessed to by
the Camps Farthest Out.

I had heard Dr. Clark's name mentioned quite often, but always
accompanied by a solemn and earnest warning to have nothing
to do with him or with the Camps Farthest Out. It was said they
taught dangerous errors that would lead people far astray from
the real truth in the inspired Scriptures and cause complete darkness and loss of God's favor and grace.

However, as I listened to Dr. Glenn Clark and to the gracious,
gentle, and loving words that proceeded from his lips and saw
the light shining from his eyes, it seemed beautifully clear that
the name of the loving Savior of all was inscribed in his forehead.
So I poured out everything that was troubling my heart to this
God-sent messenger. Then I ended by saying with sad bewilderment that, happy and thankful as I was to have jumped over a
wall and gone outside the camp into real freedom to share all
the glorious new illuminations God was giving me, it seemed
that there were no opportunities to do it. And why? Why had
physical symptoms appeared in my body, which had given those
to whom I had been witnessing the opportunity to declare far
and wide that God was clearly judging and punishing me for my
new and dangerously erroneous teachings?

Dr. Glenn Clark looked at me with a gentle, sympathetic smile
and said, "Perhaps it is to let you know that instead of feeling
hurt and wounded by the consequences of being a faithful witness, there is a better and more Jesus-like way of reacting to
them. Praise and rejoice and give thanks to God that he is leading
you 'farther on and higher up' into a new realm of heavenly light
and truth not known before. Your body is also cooperating and
wanting you to understand that from now on there must be no
more hurt thoughts and emotions, or it will cause pain to your

body also. But if you rejoice and praise God, your emotions will be healed and so will your body. Also, have only loving, understanding thoughts toward those who are so earnestly warning others not to listen to what they sincerely believe are dangerous and erroneous teachings. Then your loving sympathy will be able to help them too.

"You tell me you were taught by the Lord about the need for transformed thoughts and cleansed lips, and your body confirmed that teaching in a most beautiful and seemingly miraculous way. Now the same thing can happen as you joyfully accept this rejection by others and find yourself 'outside the camp' bearing his reproach. Very soon you will find that your body is entirely healed and filled with greater energy and life than ever before. And, who knows, perhaps you may be privileged and trusted to transmit some of the Lord's healing power to others."

What a blessed interview that was with Dr. Clark! He had obeyed God's guidance to visit, uninvited, someone he had never before heard of, and to be God's faithful messenger to me. His words were indeed inspired, and in responding to the message, by God's grace, I did experience a beautiful spiritual and complete bodily healing within a very short time.

But more than that, Dr. Clark invited me to attend a Camps Farthest Out conference to be held in Arizona, on the very edge of the Grand Canyon. They would pay my expenses there and hospitality for the whole week. At the conference I would find opportunity for blessed fellowship with others, to discover if God had some new purpose to unfold to me.

Oh, what a marvelous privilege and joy! I went to the camp on the edge of the Grand Canyon and experienced the unique fellowship of waiting on the Lord to be taught by him. And I was invited to speak at two extra sessions especially arranged for that purpose. As a result a wonderful new door of opportunity was set open before me: I was invited to be a speaker at more Camps Farthest Out.

So there opened up before me five years of the most blessed fellowship with others, seeking for more spiritual insights, light, and power. Continually I received the opportunity to learn from other Camps Farthest Out leaders glorious insights that have been an indescribable blessing ever since. At the camps I was led to understand more fully the connection between our spiritual health and holiness and the health and healing of our bodies. Also I learned more clearly that absolutely nothing happens to us by chance either in our external circumstances or in our bodies. Everything begins and is motivated by thoughts, imaginations, desires, and emotions. All our words do indeed become flesh and affect the health of our bodies; and all our actions become external happenings toward which our bodies gravitate.

At the Camps Farthest Out I spent many hours counseling with individuals, work that I had very little experience doing. God graciously taught me through the years and by the wise help of other camp leaders a series of helpful principles and teachings connected with counseling. Many of them I included in the books that I continued to write and then to sell at the bookstalls at each camp. During that period I began writing and printing the Ulpan books, [Hebrew name for daily instruction classes] which now, many years later, are being used to help readers in many different countries. These Ulpan teachings formed the messages that I was privileged to share at different camps during the next few years, along with the earlier messages now sent forth far and wide through the kind and gracious help of Tyndale House Publishers.

I owe a special debt of gratitude to two C.F.O. Leaders. One was Dr. Frank Laubach of the World Literacy Movement, and the other was Starr Daily, the transformed criminal who became one of the most loving, Jesus-like witnesses to God's saving power and forgiving love that I have ever met. Being privileged to help at camps in fellowship with them blessed and enriched me in a way hard to describe. Books written by Agnes Sanford about the connection between our thought lives and our physical health or sickness also furthered my spiritual education.

I never saw Dr. Glenn Clark again after that first camp in Arizona to which he invited me in such a wonderful way. Just a few months later he went to be with the Lord. One of his ministries during that last half-year of his life was to seek out and visit a completely unknown person undergoing an unusually testing and difficult experience. He thus opened for me a new door of far greater opportunity than ever before. What a debt of gratitude I owe to that holy, humble, gracious founder and leader! It was indeed as though the Camps Farthest Out were just like "a mercy seat of pure gold" (Exod. 25:17), where the Lord met with us. And we communed with him and were taught his loving commandments and how to make everything according to the pattern that he showed us (vv. 23–40).

22

The Cherubim on the Mercy Seat

Make images of angels, using beaten gold, and place them at the two ends ... of the Ark. ... The cherubim [angels] shall be facing each other, looking down upon the place of mercy. And I will meet you there and talk with you from above the place of mercy between the cherubim ... There I will tell you my commandments for the people of Israel.

EXODUS 25:18–22

IT SEEMED TO ME that fellowship at the Camps Farthest Out in those early days was just like fellowship in the heavenly places, about which the Apostle Paul writes so often and with such wonder and joy. Looking back in memory to that time deepens the impression of the joy of heavenly fellowship and the invisible but blessed influence of the company of the angelic hosts of heaven in the spiritual realms of love and goodness.

It is also fascinating to recall what unexpectedly blessed things were implanted in my memory at that time, making a lasting impression upon my mind and character. For instance, I recall Starr Daily helping me just like an angelic messenger at a time when I was completely inexperienced in counseling work.

One day a lady came to me asking for counsel about divorcing her husband, which she greatly desired to do. As she poured out her feelings and attitude toward her husband and described what she looked upon as his impossibly difficult and selfish behavior, with no thought whatsoever about her own unlovely attitudes and behavior to him, I began to feel sorry for the poor man to whom she was married. She finally ended her outpourings with a sharp challenge: "Well, what do you, who call yourself a spiritual counselor, advise me to do?" I paused a moment and then as kindly as I could I expressed the feeling she had awakened in my own heart. "Well, dear, perhaps if you feel like that and find him so really unlovable, it might be more helpful to you both to separate."

Then she flounced out of the room and in about an hour came hurrying back again and exclaimed impatiently, "Well really, what am I supposed to do? I ask counsel and advice from one leader at this conference and then ask the other leader for his, and he tells me to do just the opposite!"

"Oh!" I exclaimed in shame and distress. "I really am ever so sorry. You know I am very inexperienced at present in this counseling work and Starr Daily [the other leader] is a God-inspired expert at it. Don't pay any attention to what I said to you, but go by what Starr told you to do." With that she left me.

As soon as possible I sought a few moments with Starr and confessed to him my un-Christlike attitude toward the lady and my pity for her husband. He looked at me gently and then said with a kindness that I have never forgotten, and that has been like a guiding beacon to me ever since, "Hannah, don't let us ever tell anyone that they may do something that the Lord Jesus clearly stated must not be done, and that includes divorce" (Matt. 5:27–32). It is a simple and radiant truth.

On another occassion I had been listening to him speaking about one of the worst tortures that he had undergone, and I cried out, "Oh, Starr, how could you possibly bear it?" He said earnestly and sweetly, "Hannah, I discovered that if I hated enough I could bear an amazing amount of suffering. But when I came to know the Lord Jesus I found that if he helps us to love enough, it becomes possible to bear triumphantly any and every worst pain that may be inflicted upon us and even to rejoice in it."

How privileged I was to be allowed to learn from such a spirit-filled practitioner of the Kingdom of Heaven principles taught by the Lord Jesus! It seemed that angelic messengers spoke to me through the lips of Starr Daily.

Dr. Frank Laubach was outstandingly filled with the Holy Spirit. His own key message has been engraved in shining letters in my heart and my Book of Remembrance: "Say in thought and if possible in some form of action to everyone you meet, You are one of my brothers or sisters, Can I Help You?" C.I.H.U!

One other blessed acquaintance I made during those C.F.O. years led to enrichment in a fascinating way. Once, in between camps, I was invited to rest and enjoy a short holiday at a small spiritual conference center in Oregon. One morning I was sitting beside a picturesque stream of water rushing over some rocks at the foot of a tree-covered mountain. I was talking to another woman who was also staying at the conference center, and I found myself sharing with her how greatly I longed that my body should become a living temple in which the Spirit of God could dwell and which he could use in any way he chose. I recalled that at Bible college the motto had been that we were all to present ourselves to be living temples for God to dwell in, and that "the house of the Lord must be built on the top of the mountain." I told her the Camps Farthest Out had been challenging me to long to go farther on and higher up to the very top of the mount of God.

When the bell rang for luncheon, we left the stream and walked back to the dining hall. After eating the leader of the group said that we were privileged to have a special kind of blessing not planned on the program. A woman who lived near-by and who had a gift for seeing and reading auras had kindly come to see us, and if we wished we might now sit in a semicircle and let her describe and read our personal auras. We would find it a challenging and helpful experience.

I was horrified. I still had ideas impressed upon my mind during the earlier years of my Christian experience that made me suppose that anything to do with auras and extrasensory perceptions was connected with dangerous occult practices. But I am also by nature curious. I decided to stay and see what happened and ask the Lord to preserve me from any dangerous influences that might arise.

About eight of us sat in a semicircle. The woman sat facing us and closed her eyes. After she had asked a blessing of our loving heavenly Father to inspire and encourage us, she began her readings.

First, with closed eyes, she spoke to a man sitting at the end of the line. He had been brought to the conference center by his wife, who begged us to pray that he would be helped in a special way. He was a confirmed alcoholic, and, when under the influence of drink, he would beat her unmercifully and terrify the children. So all of us in the group had been praying for his deliverance.

The woman spoke aloud and said gently and happily, "Oh, sir, I see the most beautiful Christ light shining all around you. It is beautiful beyond words. How I wish that everyone could see it too, and how tenderly the Lord must love you and look upon you with special grace!"

"There you are!" I exclaimed to myself, with bitter mirth and disbelief. "Fancy seeing a beautiful Christ light emanating from an alcoholic who beats his wife in such a cruel way. That certainly does show that it is blasphemous rubbish to which we are listening."

Then the woman faced two other members in the group and declared that she saw a beautiful Christ light shining around them too. She went on to describe certain things she saw in their colored auras.

Then it was my turn, and she faced me with closed eyes and began with her usual remark. "Oh, what a beautiful light is shining around you! Your aura seems to be filled with angelic beings who are very busy about some kind of work. Yes, now I see that they are building what looks like a most beautiful temple. There it is, plainly visible in your aura. It seems to be built quite high up on the side of a very great mountain. And now I see that the angels are talking and planning together to lift it up and carry it right up to the top of the mountain and not to leave it on the lower slopes. It looks as though they are quite determined and able to do that!"

I was transfixed, though anyone could have knocked me over with a feather. It seemed that she was seeing in my aura the very words I had spoken just before luncheon. Therefore my thoughts and my words must be visibly shining all around me in some extraordinary way. It sounded like Jesus, whom we are told in the Gospels could see the thoughts of those who were speaking to him (Luke 5:22, Matt. 9:4, Matt. 12:25, Luke 6:8, 11:17).

Then the woman passed on to a gentleman I knew quite well, who attended many of the C.F.O. camps and who often led the music and singing. "Oh sir," she said, "the light shining around you is full of the most beautiful music and heavenly harmonies. I think you must love music very much, and one of your favorite composers is perhaps Tchaikovsky, for I see one of his symphonies [she named which one] sounding in your aura even now in the most beautiful way."

When she finished her aura readings, she quietly left the room, and all the group appeared to be dazed with wonder and awe.

I hurried up to the gentleman I knew whose aura was full of music and burst out to him, "Oh, do you really believe it is true that everything we think and say becomes impressed upon some kind of aura around us, which some people are actually able to see? What do you think?"

He appeared to be almost overcome by some strong emotion and then said, "Hannah, I must believe it from now on. For before I drove my wife here to this retreat this morning, while she finished getting ready, I sat down at the piano and played the particular Tchaikovsky symphony that she named."

Then I told him of my own conversation about building a temple for the Holy Spirit to use as a dwelling place, and how I longed that it would be on the top of the mountain and not on the lower slopes. And we worshiped and thanked our Father together.

After that I got to know and love the aura reader very much indeed. Her name was Tillie Baxter, and she now lives in the heavenly world, so I feel free to mention her name and to try to express how much I owe to her holy, inspiring influence.

One thing did puzzle me for a time, and at last I felt the urge to ask her about it.

"Tillie," I said, "I am absolutely bewildered about one thing. I am sure now that all our thoughts, desires, emotional patterns, and reactions are definitely impressed on some kind of invisible substance emanating from our minds and hearts. But how could you possibly see a beautiful Christ light shining around that poor alcoholic man and some of the other people here who have no personal experience of a new birth to God-consciousness, whose minds are still in spiritual darkness?"

Never can I forget her answer and the profound influence it made upon me. "Hannah, I have never in my life seen a single human being who did not have Christ's light and love shining all around them. Everyone has it. But I can also see clearly those who have not opened their hearts and minds to receive it, so they remain in inner darkness. But I long for them all to know that Christ's light and love really is there shining all around them and waiting for them to open themselves and invite him to come in."

What a glorious message that is!

The more I got to know dear Tillie the more one thing besides her gift of aura reading impressed me. I never once heard her say anything depreciative about anyone, and she never mentioned faults in other people. Every time she spoke she drew attention to something lovely, good, beautiful, helpful, inspiring, and worthy of admiration and thanksgiving. What a wonderful sight her own aura must have been! But though we could not see it, we certainly could feel it as a holy influence constantly emanating from her in a marvelous way.

It was that God-inspired habit of hers that awoke a passionate longing in me to practice the same Kingdom of Heaven attitudes, words, and deeds. I began praying not just for cleansed lips which never spoke anything negative (for that I was already seeking to practice), but for the grace always to express positive, lovely, God-inspired words, just as the Lord Jesus did whenever he spoke, with no idle or useless words among them. O my Lord, just like you when you spoke and all wondered at the gracious words that proceeded out of your lips (Luke 4:22), may that be more and more the case whenever I speak, and may I be prompted by you!

23

Show Me Thy Glory

Inside the tent the Lord spoke to Moses face to face as a man speaks to his friend. Moses talked there with the Lord and said to him ... "Please ... guide me clearly along the way you want me to travel so that I will understand you and walk acceptably before you." And the Lord replied, "I myself will go with you and give you success." ... Then Moses asked to see God's glory. The Lord replied, "I will make my goodness pass before you and I will announce to you the meaning of my name Jehovah the Lord. I show kindness and mercy to anyone I want to."

EXODUS 33:11–19

THREE OR FOUR happy years passed by in fellowship with the Camps Farthest Out, speaking at more and more of their conferences and in between writing the messages in book form and getting them printed. The speaking schedules, however, got fuller and fuller, and I began to wonder how long I would be physically able to cope with the increasing demands made upon my body and mind.

After so many years of learning to use a stammering mouth, it was now a marvelous delight to be able to speak freely and easily, and I loved the platform work. It all seemed like a daily miracle that more and more speaking invitations were arriving. But, alas, I was becoming more and more snared into love of platforms and large responsive groups rather than small ones. I realized this and continually begged the Lord to deliver me. He did so by means of yet another overwhelming experience of light pouring into my mind and understanding.

During the summer of 1960 when I was feeling very tired, a woman invited me to stay with her and rest for a week or two between camps in her beautiful home in the mountains in New Mexico. There I could go on peaceful country walks far away from crowds of people. This was just the kind of holiday place I liked best, and I happily and gratefully accepted.

Upon arrival I discovered with a shock of dismay that my hostess was what I called a "fanatical vegetarian," and she very much wanted to encourage me to become one too. I was quite determined not to become one of those cranky, misled zealots. Certainly the whole Bible was full of assurances that we humans are to eat the flesh of clean animals and poultry, with thanksgiving, and that it is the Creator's will that we should do so.

I explained this to my hostess and said that I was very sorry, but I could not stay there under those conditions. Then to my great relief she assured me that I need not leave. Her husband was not a vegetarian; he insisted on eating ordinary meals containing meat dishes of every kind, and she would willingly give me the same food that she prepared for him. It was just that she would like to interest me in altogether better food habits, which she believed would keep me from exhaustion and which would reinvigorate my body in a most blessed way. But she assured me that she would not press me and that it was a joy to have me staying in her home.

Thankfully I unpacked my things and went to bed. I had a good night's sleep and then awoke to my early morning Quiet Time. My hostess kindly brought a tray to my room so that I could have breakfast restfully in bed. And there, lying on the tray, was a little book that she said I might find interesting while I ate my breakfast. Then she left the room.

I glanced apprehensively at the little book, and, yes, apparently it was all about vegetarianism. "Oh dear!" I thought. "I shall just have to glance through it to please my kind hostess and not rudely refuse even to look at it."

So I picked up the little book, meaning to skim through it just glancing at the chapter titles.

Well, *blessed be little books*! They can act like heavenly dynamite, exploding and causing revolutionary changes in the attitudes of those who read them. God used that little book in New Mexico and once again changed the whole course of my life.

While I ate my breakfast I began reading the little book, and I could not lay it down until I had finished it. It is astounding that I cannot remember the title of the book, nor the name of the author, nor a single thing written in it. But when I laid it down I knew one thing: never again in my life could I eat any kind of meat taken from animals, fish, or birds. For just as I had already learned to the depths of my being that God our Father Creator is immanent and conscious in all human beings, so now I knew that he is equally immanent in all living creatures, from the greatest to the least, even the tiny gnats and midges. The Lord Jesus himself plainly stated this fact when he said, "Not a sparrow falls to the ground but your heavenly Father knows it." And he knows it not just by looking on from a throne far off in the heavenly realms, but by being conscious in the sparrow, feeling its pain and its vulnerability.

With that little book in my hand I realized in conviction and horror that whatever I share in doing to the other living creatures as well as to human beings, I am doing to my loving Creator Father himself. All that goes on in the slaughterhouses and by means of twentieth-century factory farming methods and in vivisection experimental laboratories is done to him. He feels and experiences it all. Day after day and year after year, throughout my whole life until that moment, I had shared in crucifying the love and consciousness of God over and over again, nailing it to the cross that we fallen human beings have made for ourselves and for all the living creatures in whom he is conscious.

Conviction of sin and of acting with cruelty to others overwhelmed me. The frightful magnitude of the tortures that we inflict upon untold billions of living creatures the world over—and therefore upon their Creator too, who breathes his own life and consciousness into all of them—appalled me. Yet the Creator continues to love and forgive us. He pleads with us to understand and seek his help and grace and to cease completely from continuing to share in the holocaust of torture. From that breakfast hour the first morning in New Mexico I knew that I could never again eat any food that had been obtained by causing suffering and death to other living creatures. I must become once more a blessed, unfallen Garden of Eden person and eat only the fruits, plants, and grain food ordained by God in Genesis 1:29. And from that hour to this I have never tasted any meat of any kind.

When my hostess returned for the breakfast tray, I told her of this decision, and she was overjoyed. For the rest of my visit, I shared her meals and not those of her husband. She taught me as much as she could about the vegetables and fruits that contain the most nourishment for ordinary human beings. But the visit was of necessity too short for me to gain anything but the barest outline of this subject. What we dwelt upon was the need to pray and seek to help others make the same revolutionary discovery too, and to long to become Holy Harmless people.

When I left I still felt ignorant about the best, easiest, and quickest way to change my eating habits and help my body adapt without too much violent opposition. I talked about it with the loving Lord, and he assured me that he would help me to do so. And he did, completely and with astonishingly little difficulty. For from the very first moment of conviction the thought of continuing to be a corpse eater sent a shudder of horror through me. By contrast, the delicious fruits, grains, and fresh vegetables on which my hostess fed me during the next few days made me realize quickly how supremely more tasty they were than dead flesh of any kind.

But I also knew at once why the little book had such a dynamic effect upon me. For deeply impressed in my memory were two special occasions when I *had* known with horror and loathing that flesh eating is an utterly brutal, even devilish, evil. Many, many years before, the message had been given to me; I knew it but could not bring myself to receive it. Instead I had willfully closed the eyes of my understanding and deafened my ears to the pleadings of the voice of conscience. This is described in the next chapter.

24

A Merciful and Gracious God

Ex 34-5,6 Then the Lord descended in the form of a pillar of cloud and stood there with him, . . . and announced the meaning of his name.

"I am the Lord, the merciful and gracious God," he said, "slow to anger and rich in steadfast love and truth."

IN THE EARLY 1940s, while I was still traveling from place to place in Palestine distributing Bibles and New Testaments, for a year or two I rented a little house on the slopes of Mount Gerizim on the outskirts of Nablus. There the last remnant of the Samaritan tribe lived and each year celebrated their annual animal sacrifice on the summit of Mount Gerizim, just as they had done since Bible times. The first summer I decided to join thousands of curious sightseers, foreign tourists, and Palestinians going to watch their celebration.

When we had walked up to the mountaintop, we found the flat summit already carpeted with soft green grass after the winter rains. Everyone belonging to the Samaritan tribe except the sick and the very aged were assembled there. All the men and boys were kneeling in a circle around a little green lawn or tiny meadow, and there grazing the soft green grass was a little flock of the most gentle and harmless creatures in the world—a number of sheep with their lambs.

Around the circle at different places great pits had been dug and filled with mountain wild brush, to act as firewood on which the sacrifices were to be cooked and then eaten all night long by the Samaritan population. Women crouched on the ground beside the pits, their children with them, and they all stared wide-eyed at the huge crowd of smartly dressed visitors and eastern Moslem people from other parts of Palestine.

About an hour before sunset the prayers, chants, and festal ceremony began, led by the high priest in his special robes calling upon Allah to bless his people and to receive their prayers and sacrifice. Then as the sun sank in a flaming red ball into the waters of the far-off Mediterranean Sea, the high priest gave the awaited signal, and every man and youth in the kneeling group seized one of the sheep or lambs and plunged a knife into its throat. Blood spurted far and wide over the worshipers and over the nearby spectators.

There was no resistance from the helpless victims. No outcry of desolate bleating was heard, only a series of long, gasping, drawn-out sighs as the gentle victims endured the agony of bleeding to death with the frightful, torturing cramps that human beings bleeding to death on battlefields experience at the hands of their enemies.

I shut my eyes to blot out the ghastly sight, and my heart throbbed and pounded with unspeakable horror. I seemed to hear over and over again these words: *"Behold! Behold! The lamb of God who bears the sins of the world!"*

Then pandemonium broke out. Even before the last gasping sighs ended, men, women, and children screamed excitedly; the bloody bodies ceased their convulsive heavings. The men began skinning them and throwing them into the burning pits, where the women watched them roast and then prepared them for a night of nonstop feasting and religious reveling.

The crowds turned away down the mountainside and dispersed. Desperately I tried to forget the scene. I told myself that it was non-Christian heathen worship, but I knew it was an annual repetition of the Old Testament sacrifices against which the faithful prophets of God had so often protested. Many times they declared that God did not desire the blood of beasts and offerings of their cooked flesh, that indeed he loathed them. For example, see Isaiah 1:11–15: "To what purpose is the multitude of your sacrifices unto me? saith the Lord. . . . I delight not in the blood of bullocks, or of lambs, or of he goats. When ye come to appear before me, who hath required this at your hand? . . . Bring no more vain oblations; incense is an abomination unto me [drowning out the stench of dead bodies]. . . . Your appointed feasts my soul hateth: they are a trouble unto me . . . Your hands are full of blood" (KJV). And so on, again and again the Old Testament prophets began to proclaim this message to the people. But Christians, just like Israel of old, pay no attention to it.

After that Passover scene, whenever I saw a truckload of cattle with terrified eyes being driven to the slaughterhouses, I turned my eyes away in horror. I knew deep within my heart that the Passover lambs had breathed out with their dying gasps the truth that men and women, made in the image and likeness of God, act like heartless devils in their attitude and behavior toward other living creatures. But I had never dared to face the fact honestly or to ask our heavenly Creator what he really thinks about it and what he longs for us to understand.

Long before the Samaritan sacrifice, when still a small child, the truth had been drawn to my attention. During the First World War my father began to keep a number of big brown rabbits in hutches in a shed on our large paddock. He gave me a special gift: a big, snowy white, pink-eyed rabbit to be my very own pet. I was such a desolate child with a stammering mouth and no

human friends, but in Peter, the white rabbit, I found an absolutely perfect friend. I loved him with my whole lonely heart,
and he adored me. I would take him out of his special hutch and
hug him, and he would cuddle close to me with his long white
ears twitching gently against my cheek. He just loved being
picked up and hugged, and when I put him down he would
follow me wherever I went and come when I called his name.
He would tell me in every possible way that I was the delight of
his life just as he was of mine. It was like a Garden of Eden
friendship with the animal kingdom all over again. It lasted all
throughout one long beautiful summer.

Then one day when I went out to the hutch to take my friend
Peter for his daily walk, to my consternation the hut was empty.
I walked all over the paddock calling his name, but he had vanished. Presently the dinner bell rang, and I ran into the house to
get ready for the meal. We sat down around the table in the large
dining room, and there was a moment or two of silent Quaker
grace and thanks for the food that we were about to receive from
our heavenly Father. Then the door opened and in came one of
Mother's wartime helpers carrying a great covered dish smoking
hot from the oven. When the cover was removed, there was a
whole roast rabbit ready for us to eat. And oh! It was my best
friend Peter rabbit, offered up as a victim on the altar of food
shortages and wartime rationing.

As soon as I realized the frightful truth, I rushed from the
room screaming and sobbing with heartbroken sorrow and despair that I could not and would not eat anything from that great
awful dish. My one and only friend had gone. I would never be
able to hold him in my arms again and feel him snuggling so
lovingly against me and his long soft ears brushing against my
cheeks.

They called to me to come back, but I screamed, "I can't! I
can't eat my best friend! Oh, I have lost him forever." With the

best intentions in the world they compelled me to return and to eat a few mouthfuls of his flesh, telling me that he would be happy to sacrifice himself for us, who had been so kind to him, and to supply us with food when rations were so hard to come by.

But I knew better. Even as a little child I knew that we must never willfully and cruelly sacrifice our friends and never, never nourish our own bodies by killing them and depriving them of life.

So there on the mountaintop in New Mexico in 1960 I realized that my precious rabbit and the lambs on Mount Gerizim had not died in vain. They spoke their heartbreaking message as unresistingly they were put to death: that what we do to them, we are really doing to ourselves too, and that the time will come when our own bodies will be killed and eaten by disease and death just as we killed and ate them. But far, far more awful even than that: what we do to them we also do to their Creator and ours. He feels it all and bears it and forgives it. This is what the slaughtered animals tell us, and through their shed blood and writhing bodies they send forth a call to our inmost being.

"Behold, behold the Lamb of God who bears and forgives the sins of the whole world!"

Yes, that morning in New Mexico, the truth was revealed to me. And what the Holy Spirit causes us to see we can never unsee! From that morning to this not a single morsel of flesh have I eaten, but only Garden of Eden plant food once again. Glory be to God for the blessed Book of Memory and the priceless treasures it contains!

25

The Lord Will Do Marvels

Seeking to live according to the Garden of Eden standard

*Moses ... bowed his head toward the earth and worshipped.
And he said, If now I have found grace in thy sight, O Lord, let
my Lord, I pray thee, go among us ... and pardon our ... sin,
and take us for thine inheritance. And he said, Behold, I make
a covenant: ... I will do marvels. ... and all the people ... shall
see the work of the Lord.*

EXODUS 34:8–10 KJV

ONCE AGAIN this new illumination immediately started another
revolution in my life, not only in my own personal way of living,
but also in all my circumstances. Everything seemed to begin
grinding to a halt all over again. As soon as the rest time in New
Mexico ended, I discovered that this new insight about Holy
Harmlessness and return to the Garden of Eden plant food, when
I tried to share it with others, proved to be the most unpopular
of messages.

I found this as soon as I arrived at the next C.F.O. camp. At
meals I quietly stopped taking flesh of any kind and said nothing.
Instead I ate fruit, vegetables, and bread. As soon as people began noticing this they naturally asked why, and there was quiet
but strong disapproval. Just as when I first went "outside the
camp" of my earnest evangelical friends, so now all further invitations to continue speaking at the C.F.O. camps came to an
end.

How strange it is that the most tender-hearted, loving followers of the Lord Jesus seem to reject this message of never harming the living creatures even more than ordinary irreligious people do. It seems that just because they are so loving and tender-hearted they dare not face up to the awful fact that the horrors they pay other human beings to do to the fish, poultry, and animals also is being done to their own loving heavenly Father. It is too awful an idea to consider for even one moment. So they at once thankfully insist that the Bible is full of verses concerning the animal sacrifices that were to be offered to God and then eaten by those who offered them. So it must be God's will for us to eat flesh too. But they forget, or are never reminded of the fact, that the sacrifices ordained in the Mosaic law were only God's permissive will and not his ideal wish for his chosen people. It was permitted because in the wilderness the people fiercely demanded, "Give us flesh to eat or we will go back to Egypt." So Moses was told to permit them to eat the flesh of clean (harmless, not flesh-eating) animals until they could be persuaded to accept his ideal will. And it is clearly stated that their stubborn rejection of God's appointed food of manna instead of flesh caused their bodies to become subject to grievous diseases just like those of the flesh-eating Egyptians.

When the last camp appointment was finished I found myself once again bereft of all opportunities to witness at meetings and conferences, but not this time without financial means. I had received generous gratuities at all the C.F.O. camps as well as hospitality in between them.

So I returned to England and to the Christian guest house in my old home and to the loving-kindness of my stepmother, though she too did not feel able to accept the new message. I waited quietly on the Lord, asking to be shown his new plan, now that once again all platform witness had vanished and all the doors were closed. With him I looked back over the way he had led thus far; and at all the altars of obedient surrender that I had been learning to build.

The first altar had been built at Keswick in 1924 when I yielded my stammering mouth and was led to study at Bible college.

The second altar was built in 1921, when I was asked to appear as a fool for Christ's sake and to travel about the British Isles witnessing in the villages.

The third had been built at Ireland's Eye when the call came to go as a missionary to Palestine, and later to distribute Bibles and New Testaments all over the country.

The fourth altar called me to become hospital housekeeper and then to stay in Jerusalem through the siege.

The fifth in 1950 caused me to yield my lips to cleansed and transformed thoughts.

The sixth called me to be an arrow in God's quiver and to be shot from land to land around the world.

The seventh was built when I went outside the camp bearing his reproach and was confronted with nothing but closed doors, until the wonderful new opening.

The eighth called me to begin witnessing joyfully with the Camps Farthest Out and to enjoy all the privileges entailed in that work.

And now the ninth altar: the call to become a Holy Harmless Garden of Eden person again (Heb. 7:26, Phil. 2:15, Matt. 10:16).

Each altar of surrender had led to greater opportunity than ever before. "So now," said the loving Lord, "you are joyfully to learn still a new kind of witness under my direction. It is to be *person-to-person work*, witnessing to individuals who will be ready and longing to hear what you have to share with them."

"But how can I find such people, Lord?" I asked. "They don't seem to exist anywhere. No one with whom I am in contact wants to hear about Holy Harmlessness."

"Just trust me," said the Lord, "and I will bring them to you."

Then he led me to buy a big second-hand house trailer parked on a little island just ten miles away from my home town. I was to spend six months of each year there to prepare my own harmless meals. And I was to continue writing little booklets, which I was to get printed and to distribute freely to anyone who wanted to receive them. At the same time the Lord put me in contact with a reader and his wife who were wonderfully kind, and a printer in my home town who turned out to be the most loyal friend and helper, printing the booklets inexpensively and storing them at the print shop. The printer's wife, with marvelous kindness, sent them to all who wrote asking for them while I was away from the trailer.

For the other six months of the year the Lord wished me to spend back in Israel. He gave me a lovely three-room cottage there, high on the hills above the Sea of Galilee. There I could not only continue writing, but could once again use a little car and drive about giving lifts to people waiting at the side of the road, and so have the opportunity to speak to them individually with no indignant on-lookers.

When I moved into the house trailer on the little island, the Lord gave me a completely new ministry—this time to the children on the trailer site. I had never done children's work before, nor had I wanted to. I had been so unhappy myself as a child that I had always avoided contact with children, telling myself that I did not know how to get on with them. But now in a most wonderful way one of the most joyous forms of witness was opened up before me.

One little mentally retarded boy and a little girl friend of his were the first two children with whom the Lord put me in touch. I began taking them for walks along the seashore, talking to them about the birds and sea creatures, the crabs and jellyfish. We watched the animals lovingly and tried to understand what they were expressing by their different forms of behavior. We asked them why they ran and flew away whenever they saw human beings getting near them. I began writing and telling stories about this, and bit by bit more children watched and listened and then began coming to the house trailer on Sunday mornings for Sunday school classes. Presently there were nearly twenty of them, and the trailer almost exploded as I played choruses and they sang them and banged toy cymbals and little musical instruments of all kinds. What happy times we had! Then a few of their parents became interested and read the little books I had been writing. So the months passed with happy opportunities and less physical strain than I had ever before experienced.

Then to my astonished delight, during the winter months in Israel, I was able to start Sunday school classes for some of the missionaries' children in Galilee. I shared the same stories and messages that I had been writing and teaching, about being kind, happy friends with all the birds and beasts, just as the Lord Jesus had been. How happy it makes our heavenly Father when we make friends with them and never hurt them in any way!

It was nearly twenty-five years ago that I was privileged to begin witnessing to the children, and some of them who are now parents tell me that they have never forgotten some of those stories and the lasting impressions made on them. As for me, I discovered with wonder and delight how true the blessed words of the Lord Jesus are: "He that receiveth one of these little ones in my name, receiveth me." Sunday after Sunday I knew his presence in a more radiant and joyful way than at any other time.

26

The Presence of God

Confirming signs that "The Harmless cannot be harmed."

Moses didn't realize as he came back down the mountain with the tablets that his face glowed from being in the Presence of God. Because of this radiance upon his face Aaron and the people were afraid to come near him . . . the people would see his face aglow.

EXODUS 34:29, 30, 35

While these new events were taking place in my life, I was also learning more and more from the Lord about how to live a Garden of Eden life without eating meat of any kind. Soon I gave up eating all dairy food because of the cruelties involved in Twentieth-century factory farming methods. Then I was led to stop wearing clothing made from wool because so much came from sheep shorn before they were taken to the slaughterhouse. Also, I wore no leather shoes or boots and used no leather bags or suitcases, because leather, like furs and skins of all kinds, is obtainable only by slaughtering other creatures.

It is written in Exodus 28 that all the garments worn by the priests were to be made from linen or cotton, with no admixture of wool or skin of any kind. "Thou shalt make holy garments. . .for glory and for beauty" (V.2). Then verses 4, 5, 8, 15, 39, and twice in 42 emphasize seven times over that the holy garments must be made of linen only. How much there was for me to learn and to share with others! During that time God put me in touch with a few people who did want to learn about this Holy Harmless life. Two people in England by this means became special friends of mine and faithful helpers through all the ensuing years even until now, and their fellowship and loving friendship and witness have been a great blessing and encouragement to me.

One particular reassurance was given to me, which I remember with special gratitude. I was staying in my house trailer at the time in England, and one day I received a newspaper cutting sent to me from friends in the United States. It made the shattering statement that scientists and research workers were now discovering that plants also have feelings and can suffer pain. It claimed that tomatoes send out a response that seems like shrieks of fear and anguish when they are picked and thrown into boiling water or fat.

I was appalled, for surely that must mean that we human beings cannot eat plant food as well as animal food without causing suffering and destruction. Then what can we eat in order to keep our bodies alive? Whatever was I to do? It seemed that there was nothing that I could eat harmlessly at all. Must I really let myself starve to death?

It so happened that when I read that newspaper cutting I had just eaten a substantial and satisfying vegetarian supper. But what about my fruit breakfast tomorrow?

"O Lord," I begged, "please, please speak to me and help me. It says in Genesis 1:29 that God said that all human beings as well as the animals and birds were to eat plant food. But how can that be right if the plants suffer pain when cooked and their leaves and fruit are forcibly taken away from them?"

Then the loving Lord seemed to say gently, "Don't get all upset and worried about this, Hannah. I will explain it all to you and make it quite clear. Just go to sleep now and trust me."

He enabled me to do so. I got up the next morning and dressed and took my bucket to the faucet a little further down the field, for none of the house trailers had running water.

On the way back I met a man coming out of a trailer near my own. It had arrived just the evening before, about the time I read the newspaper cutting. The man greeted me in a friendly way and asked some questions about the facilities, and then we started a conversation. He told me that he was a market gardener and had come here for a few days' holiday.

"A market gardener!" I exclaimed. Yes, he said, he grew fruits and vegetables to sell in one of the London open air markets.

I was nearly overcome and then found myself pouring out to him all about the newspaper cutting I had just received, which claimed that plants have feelings and suffer pain at what we do to them just as animals do. I was a vegetarian, I told him, and did he really think that it caused the plants agony to be picked and eaten?

I feared that he would think I was quite mad, but he listened kindly, paused a moment, and then said with a reassuring smile, "I think perhaps I can tell you something that will comfort you. I well know that a time comes when the fruits and vegetables are ripe on the plants that I grow, and that if I don't pick them the plants themselves will cause them to drop off and fall to the ground, or the birds will come and carry them away. The plants are actually longing at that time to be freed from the fruits and seeds. We help them, and the creatures help them too, because it is their nature to long to give away and share the fruits they bear at the right time. Perhaps it may hurt them to be pulled up and cut to pieces and thrown away at the wrong time of year. I don't know about that, but when we prune them properly and help them to fulfill the purpose for which they live, then we may be sure they are happy and thankful that we help them to give away freely a part of themselves to be of benefit to others, without hurting them in any way."

Oh, the joy and wonderful relief of it! It was a miracle of the Lord's perfect timing to send an unknown market gardener to help me at the precise time of my need and perplexity. I went into the trailer bubbling over with delight and had one of the most delicious fruit breakfasts that I have ever eaten.

So the years slipped by, and presently God provided me with a lovely little bungalow just across the road from the trailer site, so that the children could still come to Sunday school. I also had a place to which I could invite individuals who received my circular letters and the little booklets. They could come and stay with me for a few days, and we could have fellowship together and wait on the Lord, asking him to give us still more guidance concerning harassing problems that the visitors were dealing with. And there visitors could practice harmless cooking and learn more about how to be Holy Harmless Garden of Eden people themselves.

Again and again we read the beautiful verses in Isaiah 11: "In that day the wolf and the lamb will lie down together, and the leopard and goats will be at peace. . .Calves and fat cattle will be safe among lions, and a little child shall lead them all. The cows will graze among bears; cubs and calves will lie down together, and lions will eat grass like the cows. Babies will crawl safely amongst poisonous snakes, and a little child who puts his hand in a nest of deadly adders will pull it out unharmed. Nothing will hurt or destroy in all my holy mountain, for as the waters fill the sea, so shall the earth be full of the knowledge of the Lord" (vv. 6–9 LB).

It is a wondrous picture of the time when all human beings will be a nation of holy priests serving the Lord. When they come forth from their times of communion with him, their faces will glow with the glory of his presence just as the verses in Exodus

34 at the beginning of this chapter tell us. People everywhere will be afraid with holy dread to cause harm to others.

That was indeed the wonderful lesson that I learned during those ten or eleven years. I will trust and not be afraid, for the Lord is showing me in truly wonderful ways that *the harmless cannot be harmed*.

One experience I remember with thanksgiving and praise. As I lived and witnessed person to person, it happened that one day I was enjoying a long walk by myself on a beach where no people were anywhere in sight and no dwelling places were anywhere near. The beach was completely deserted for several miles in wild, desolate country. A dense, tangled thicket of bushes and trees grew all along the shore of the beach, and I seemed to be alone in an empty world.

Then suddenly out of the thicket an almost totally naked man leaped out and rushed toward me, shouting the most obscene words about what he meant to do with my body before he killed me.

I was all alone. Not a soul was in sight. I stood paralyzed with fear and horror, unable to move or utter a sound.

Then just as the would-be rapist got almost within reach and stretched out his arms to seize me, the most beautiful, tender, loving voice I have ever heard sounded close beside me and said, "May God be merciful to you, my poor brother. He loves you so much and longs to help you."

The man stopped dead in his tracks, his wild eyes staring. "What's that?" he blurted out. And the tender voice said again, "Oh my poor brother, may God have mercy upon you; he loves you so much."

Then the poor naked madman suddenly turned around and rushed back into the thicket and I saw him no more. He acted as though he were utterly afraid to come any nearer and do anything to harm me.

Who had spoken those beautiful, loving words with such miraculous power? I only know that I heard them coming from my own lips, spoken by a holy, loving power and presence, who came and used my paralyzed lips in order to express a tender compassion that was wholly divine.

Over and over again since the Lord began teaching me about Holy Harmlessness in 1960 has the glorious truth been impressed upon me: *the harmless cannot be harmed*, neither in perils on the road, nor in perils from storms, tornadoes, hurricanes, nor from exploding shells or snipers' bullets, nor from destructive forces still at war in the Middle East, nor from sickness and disease. This is a stupendous fact and delivers us from fear of any kind.

I have also discovered that if we are tempted to compromise and begin to disobey any of our Lord's commands—by sometimes eating food or using materials and appliances obtained by causing pain and death to the other creatures, or by choosing to disregard at certain times some heavenly principle taught by the Lord Jesus in the Sermon on the Mount—that our invulnerability to harm and danger comes to an end temporarily; we can be harmed and perhaps suffer even more than do people who have less light and continually break the royal Law of Love. The Lord is wonderful, teaching us, warning us, and helping us learn to love cooperating with God's laws at all times. Thus we create only blessed experiences for ourselves and can share them with others also.

"Sing to the Lord, for he has done wonderful things and that my soul knoweth right well. Make known his praise around the world. ... For great and mighty is the Holy One of Israel who lives among you" (Isa. 12:5 LB).

May everyone see and experience the glow of his presence with us and feel a holy dread that makes them afraid to do any harm to any living creature.

27

Holiness in the Lord

The Lord said, "All right, This is the contract I am going to make with you. I will do miracles. . . . Your part of the agreement is to obey all my commandments; . . . Be very, very careful never to compromise . . . with the people there in the land where you are going, for if you do you will soon be following their evil ways."

This is what the Lord has commanded. All of you who wish to, all those with generous hearts, may bring . . . offerings to Jehovah. . . . Come, all of you who are skilled craftsmen having special talents, and construct what God has commanded us.

So all the people went to their tents to prepare their gifts. Those whose hearts were stirred by God's Spirit returned with their offerings. . . . So every man and woman who wanted to assist in the work given to them by the Lord . . . brought their free will offerings to him.

Finally the workmen all left their task to meet with Moses and told him, "We have more than enough materials on hand now to complete the job."

EXODUS 34:10–12; 35:4–29; 36:5

AFTER SEVERAL YEARS of quiet and happy but often difficult work in England and in the State of Israel during the winter months of each year, the Lord unexpectedly opened another door of new opportunities and step by step revealed the method by which the new ministry was to be carried on. I received an

invitation to return to the United States again and to begin sharing the later messages and lessons that the Lord had been teaching me.

This new ministry, he emphasized, was to be carried on in his
Secret Service, with no publicity or advertisement of any kind.
Also I was not to depend upon special organizations or financial
remunerations. In fact, it was to be just like the method taught
by the Lord Jesus to his disciples. He told them to go two by two
to every place where he himself wanted his message to be taken.
They were to go forth and preach the gospel of good news
around the whole world.

He told them that they were not to make any special arrangements for holding meetings in different places but were to wait
until the Holy Spirit opened doors of opportunity and led them
just where he wanted them to go, because people in those places
were ready and longing to hear the message and to respond to
it. Day by day where they lived and worked for a living, they
were to practice and demonstrate the Kingdom of Heaven principles that the Lord Jesus had taught them. As long as they continued to do this by God's grace, the people around them would
see God's beautiful acts of loving-kindness and the miraculous
power that results from unbroken contact with him and obedience to his will. Miracles of all kinds would begin to take place
secretly—never worked openly in front of a crowd. There would
be individual healings in homes, deliverances, release from fear,
depression, and nervous breakdown; solutions to impossible-
looking problems would be granted.

The individuals thus helped would personally but eagerly tell
others and be urged, "Each one teach one!" Then quietly, with
no display or advertisement, more and more doors would open,
and invitations would come, accompanied by offers of free hospitality and travel expenses. All this is exactly what happened
after Pentecost. The disciples received invitations from country
after country in the East and also in Europe, from those who had

attended the Jerusalem festival and experienced the power of the Holy Spirit through the preaching of the gospel.

That was God's ideal plan, a beautiful hidden Secret Service carried on in the power of the Holy Spirit. It attracted no antagonism and persecution because it went on unknown to the worldly people all around.

We read in the Acts of the Apostles that it was Peter who first embarked upon the method of publicity, in order to allow large crowds of people to be encouraged to come and listen to the gospel messages. But the majority quite likely were not ready to respond in faith to what he taught. Many wanted to contradict and denounce and condemn. Soon Peter was arrested and beaten. Then he used his miraculous power in a destructive way by causing deceitful Ananias and Sapphira to drop down dead, instead of helping them to repent and be restored. Later he was thrown into prison and was about to be killed when he was miraculously delivered by an angel (Acts 12:1–17). By that means he learned this vitally important lesson about Secret Service— not seeking to draw huge crowds of unprepared people to listen. We know this because from Acts 12:17 to the end of the book, we read no more about Peter and his ministry. After that it must all have been carried on quietly in a hidden way, just as the Lord Jesus had instructed in Matthew 10.

This method was taught and practiced by the Lord Jesus himself, after great crowds had gathered to listen and then had temporarily dispersed. He always went away quietly without telling anyone where he was going next. That prevented persecution breaking out and causing suffering to those who had responded to the message. The new converts were not tempted through fear and lack of experience of God's love and protective care to cease following the Lord.

So this method the Lord plainly told me was the right one to follow. People who had been helped by the unpublished free booklets sent out twice a year now began sending invitations to go and give Ulpan classes in their homes where they and their friends could learn still more. So a new, blessed ministry began, carried on in private homes with no advertisement of any kind.

Also another new and happy development was revealed. God had laid upon the hearts of certain people a desire to offer their help in the service of the book ministry. Rahamah was the first one to do this. She volunteered to do all the typing and the secretarial work and to use her special talents in the service of the Lord. In a most beautiful way she has continued to do so ever since. Another lovely friend opened her home, where I could stay at any time and rest, and where I could leave all the many things too cumbersome to travel with from place to place. In that way they were always available when needed, including many of the little booklets we printed.

At the beginning of this period of visiting the United States for several months each year, I still continued spending the winter months in my God-given cottage in Israel. There I got a number of copies of one of the little booklets that had been written for Jews and Arabs printed both in Hebrew and Arabic, and I distributed it in many places. This was my special joy.

However, a great many temptations were connected with this work. One was my growing, passionate desire to be released from the burden of work involved in not only writing the books but also getting them printed. The costs of printing and distributing the books mounted fantastically, and my desire for release from the burden grew stronger and stronger. At last, alas, I persuaded myself to believe that the time had come for me to seek public help in a way the Lord had told me not to do. So I prepared to sit down and write a letter that I hoped would result in publicity for the books. But thanks be to God for his kindness! He prevented me from backsliding in such a tragic way. For before I could write the letter I slipped on a wet stone floor, and

Holy Harmless as I hoped I was learning to be, I crashed head-long to the floor and lay in pain. I was picked up and laid on the bed, and a kind minister friend came and laid hands on me and prayed for healing and release from the pain. The pain did not go, but wonderful grace and power to bear it was granted almost at once.

I realized immediately why the accident had happened, and I repented wholeheartedly, and a most wonderful thing happened. I was unwilling to have a doctor because I knew that as a harmless person I could not follow all his instructions if they included taking painkillers and drugs of any kind. But when after three weeks the pain still persisted, friends persuaded me to visit a bone specialist. He took an X ray and said I had fractured my femur and in the usual way would be lying in plaster for many weeks. But he held up his hands in amazement and also exclaimed that it was the first perfect fracture he had seen in many years of practice. He wished all his students could see it too. For the two broken ends were in perfect alignment, and if not displaced in any way they would be able to grow together again of themselves. So if I insisted on refusing treatment, he would prescribe for me two special walking sticks with padded points that would not slip on the ground. With their aid I could use the one foot and get about for a few weeks in that way while the broken ends healed and joined together again. But beware! If I slipped or fell, the fracture would be very serious indeed.

For a few weeks I hobbled about with two splendid sticks supporting me, and soon, with a bag of booklets on my shoulders, I was able to drive the car and continue distributing books from door to door while the fracture gradually healed. I have never felt any effects of it since. It was another wondrous confirmation of harmlessness, and a faithful, loving warning against any kind of backsliding and compromise. Yes, I had been taught an important lesson, summed up perfectly in the verse quoted at the beginning of this chapter: *"Be very, very careful never to compromise"* (Exod. 34:12 LB).

Also a new passionate love for and joy in the Lord's Secret Service filled my heart. How true it is that all the time there are new lessons for us to learn at the right time and in the way that the Lord sees will be best!

As the years slipped by, filled with more and more visits and opportunities to witness in his Secret Service to small groups of interested people, in many different places, I found one important fact connected with Holy Harmlessness of which I had remained in complete ignorance. I learned it through my own experience and so was able to warn others and prevent them having to learn it in a difficult way themselves.

In 1964 I had become a fruitarian, eating only fruits and a little bread and nothing else. Three or four years later I developed a severe deficiency symptom, and I nearly passed out of earth life altogether. But once again the loving Lord intervened. A kind and skillful man was put in touch with me, and he prescribed just what I needed. He explained that it is absolutely essential to eat grains as well as fruits and vegetables. Then I discovered in my Hebrew Bible that the word in Genesis 1:29 translated as "seeds" is the Hebrew word for grains! So there it was, right at the beginning of the Bible. God's ideal rule for our perfect physical nourishment is plant food, including all the grains such as wheat, rye, barley, oats, and rice. My new adviser was of Eastern extraction, and he told me to remain on a diet of boiled rice only for three weeks. I expected to loathe the sight of boiled rice ever after, but instead it became one of my favorite grains, and it certainly met my urgent need marvelously.

The result was wonderful. Steadily I recovered strength, and now, years later, there are no signs of deficiency at all. A doctor who had to give me certain health tests before I could be granted

an important visa told me he could find nothing wrong anywhere.

Let us continually praise our loving heavenly Father, who so
joyfully supplies all our needs and seems to find his greatest
delight in teaching us new and wonderful things. It is marvelous
that Mother Earth freely brings forth everything that we need to
nourish our bodies and maintain them in holy health, provided
that our minds and spirits enjoy holy health too as we daily
practice the Kingdom of Heaven principles taught by the Lord
Jesus. If we fail to do that and compromise in any way, even the
wisest and most skillful health specialists will not be able to
protect us from disease and suffering. But if we live as the Lord
Jesus taught and demonstrated is the ideal way ordained by our
Father God, we shall experience blessed health for spirit, soul,
and body. Our bodies will become more and more completely
like "a holy tabernacle or temple and dwelling place for God."

As Paul tells us in 1 Cor 3.16 "Know ye not that Ye are the
temple of God, and the Spirit of God dwelleth in you." (KJV)

28

The Glory of the Lord
Filled the Tabernacle

*Moses erected the enclosure surrounding the tent and the altar,
and set up the curtain-door at the entrance of the enclosure. So
at last Moses finished the work. Then the cloud covered the tabernacle and the glory of the Lord filled it. . . . Whenever the cloud
lifted and moved the people of Israel journeyed onward and
followed it. But if the cloud stayed, they stayed until it moved.
The cloud rested upon the tabernacle during the day-time, and
at night there was fire in the cloud so that all the people of Israel
could see it. This continued throughout all their journeys.*

EXODUS 40:33–38

SO THE YEARS slipped quietly past, full of many challenging tests
and happy witness. In England I enjoyed joyous companionship
with the children and with visitors at the Holy Harmless bungalow. Then six months of each year I traveled in the United States,
lovingly and faithfully assisted by God-given friends. More and
more of the messages were also printed in manuscript form or
as little booklets which could be shared with others.

So the time of my eightieth birthday arrived, and the loving
Lord challenged me to peruse with him the pages of the precious
Book of Memory. What a wondrous joy it has been to do so—to
review the main spiritual messages learned during my time here
in the School of Earth Experience!

Now it seems as though, after long journeys in the wilderness of this poor fallen world, following as it were a cloud, representing the loving, enlightening, guiding, and protecting presence of God's Holy Spirit, I have indeed been led into a land where all God's promises are being fulfilled. The wonder and joy of it are indescribable.

Here in this Land of Fulfilled Promises there is time and opportunity to study and feed on the fruits of the trees of knowledge growing in God's holy and inspired Word. Now every page in the Bible seems to shine with fuller, deeper, and richer meanings than I have ever been able to see in them before. Verse after verse opens a door or window, revealing aspects of the Eternal Realms of Truth that hitherto had remained invisible. All the promises given by God over the years are unfolding into fulfillment in glorious ways I could never have imagined. And always I enjoy the blessed and wonderful hope that the coming of the Lord in glory is nearer than ever before, and the daily blissful delight of being on the watch for his appearance.

Ten years ago, just after I reached my seventieth birthday, I was privileged to meet a wonderful woman who was more than ninety years old. Eagerly I asked her if she had found that when one passes the "three score years and ten" period of life, one of necessity begins to go downhill in a physical and mental way. Did that happen also to one's spiritual consciousness and power, as so many people seem to think will be the case?

With a face shining with radiant, contented happiness, she replied, "Oh no! Indeed, no." That certainly had not happened to her. For all the time she still found that she was increasing in spiritual growth and vigor, with ever-greater awareness of God's presence and loving-kindness. He was becoming more precious and lovely than anything she had known before. The best and most satisfying spiritual experiences were happening to her in her nineties. And our heavenly homeland was beginning to shine all around her. Her heavenly body, which had been developing around her ever since she had been born again to God-consciousness, was now ready to be used when the time came for her to lay aside her physical one.

Then she looked at me lovingly and thoughtfully and added that she believed that our Lord was telling her that she might now share with me a wonderful spiritual reality. She was discovering that even now our loving Lord was teaching her how to use her heavenly body even while she was still on earth. She was no longer bound completely to the physical one but could move about invisibly in her spiritual one.

Oh, what a profoundly wonderful testimony she was privileged to give! She did not witness publicly or before great crowds, but she attested to the fact to individuals who had been led to her day by day by her Lord.

As I looked at her beautiful shining face, so completely freed from self-consciousness and radiant with awareness of God-consciousness, I knew that what she said must be true. Like Moses after his communion day by day in the tabernacle, face to face with the Shechinah glory of God's presence and love, her face glowed with the light of that presence, and it streamed forth from her to individuals with whom she was brought into contact.

Even so Lord Jesus! We beg you to fill us all, day by day, with more and more of the fullness of our Father's loving-kindness and tender mercy and with his enabling power to pour forth blessings into all the empty, sorrowful, and lonely lives around us.

So now for the present I close these pages of God-given messages inscribed in the Book of my Memory. I have longed to sum up in this Book of Remembrance all the truths that God, by his Holy Spirit, taught me so tenderly through the years. Others perhaps will be able to read them and find blessing, for the Savior himself lovingly and earnestly emphasized his desire in these words:

"Ye shall be witnesses unto me."

May he use this book to be a real witness to him.

The Lessons Learned in My Lifetime

Chapter 1: Thou Shalt Remember (Deut. 8:2)

THE SCHOOL OF EARTHLY EXPERIENCES

1. We come to experience life here on earth in order to:
learn humility;
be tested;
find out how we respond to God's will;
learn whether we will really obey him or not;
learn that real life comes from obeying every command of God.

Chapter 2: The Land of Bondage and Affliction (Exod. 3:7, 8)

THE YEARS OF CHILDHOOD AND GIRLHOOD

2. No one can find real satisfaction and true happiness until they find it in God alone.

3. Without being aware of God's love and presence with us, this mortal life becomes utterly desolate.

4. Despair and misery awaken yearnings in our hearts for God and start us seeking to find him and make contact with him.

Chapter 3: The Passover From Bondage Into Liberty (Exod. 13:3)

KESWICK 1924

5. We make contact with God by building altars of surrender to his will, on which we lay down our own will and yield it to him.

6.   Faith is believing what God says and being willing to do what he tells us.

Chapter 4: Manna in the Wilderness (Deut. 8:2)

THE YOUNG PEOPLE'S MEETING AT KESWICK

7.   Daily early morning Quiet Times with God, feeding upon the inspired teachings in the Bible and asking him to explain them, are the means by which we grow in grace and spiritual development.

8.   Always talk to the Lord Jesus in thought or aloud, exactly as we would if we could see him visibly present with us.

9.   Ninety-nine percent of the cases of loss of God-consciousness are due to failure to keep enjoying a daily Quiet Time with the Lord. Claim the same experience enjoyed by the prophet who said about God's love and grace, "He wakeneth me morning by morning to hear his voice" (Clarence Foster).

10.   Learn by heart each morning something said or taught by the Lord Jesus, and then go out and practice it all day long. The result will be real spiritual growth and development.

Chapter 5: The Pillar of Cloud and Pillar of Fire (Exod. 13:21, 22)

THE HOLIDAY AT KESWICK AND THE RETURN HOME

11.   Like David, take a pebble promise from God and claim it, and every giant straddling across the way will fall headlong to the ground in utter helplessness.

12.   Never say "I can't." Instead, say "God can"; so "I can do all things through Christ who strengtheneth me" (Phil. 4:13).

13.   There is one of God's rainbow promises in every storm cloud reminding us that he has promised never to leave us nor to forsake us (Heb. 13:5, 6).

14.   Handicaps are potentially our greatest blessings. They are God-given protections in disguise, and they keep us depending utterly upon the Lord.

Chapter 6: Crossing the Red Sea (Exod. 14:13–31)

RIDGELANDS BIBLE COLLEGE

15.   God says to all weak and frightened souls, "My grace is sufficient for thee, for my strength is made perfect in weakness" (2 Cor. 12:9).

16.   Take the first step in obedience, and God's enabling power will make all things possible.

17.   The angels of the Lord encamp round about those who seek to do God's will, protecting them all the time so that no evil can befall them.

18.   Don't let anything hinder you from doing what God tells you he wants you to do.

19.   Just as all the wise birds know, scarecrows always have the choicest blessings growing close beside them. Remember that a scarecrow in the way is really like an invitation to a special feast of joy and love (Frank Boreham).

20.   Fearful people are fortunate, for they have so many opportunities to let the Lord change their fear into faith.

21.   Our Lord is of tender compassion to those who are afraid (John Bunyan).

Chapter 7: The Bitter Waters at Marah (Exod. 15:22-23)

THE FRIENDS' EVANGELISTIC BAND

22. Be joyfully willing to become a fool for Christ's sake.

23. "Not many wise . . . not many mighty, not many noble are called. But God hath chosen the foolish things of the world to confound the wise; and God hath chosen the weak things of the world to confound the things that are mighty. And base things of the world, and things that are despised hath God chosen, *yea,* and things which are not, to bring to naught things that are" (1 Cor. 1:26–28 KJV).

24. Be glad and rejoice when the time comes to undergo "a dunging process," for that will help us to bear much more fruit to God's glory.

25. The motto for soldiers of Christ is RFA—Ready For Anything.

Chapter 8: The Twelve Springs at Elim (Exod. 15:27)

MORE LESSONS IN THE BAND

26. It is sometimes said, "Never say why to God." *Why* must we never say why to the Lord? Very likely God's answer will be, "Ask as many questions as you like, for you will never learn very much if you do not do so. But never ask why in a whining voice such as, 'Oh God, *why* did you let this horrible thing happen to me? It is most unfair and unkind of you.'"

27. Often God allows us to have thorns pricking us instead of eyes by which to see the way. For a hedge of thorns along the narrow path will help us not to wander away from his will for us.

28.   The wilderness can be made to rejoice and blossom like the rose, and the desert can become a garden full of blooming flowers if we accept all disagreeable things believing that they are begging us to transform them into their opposite, good things (Isa. 35).

29.   Never say no to God, but always a happy yes.

30.   "Your heavenly Father will abundantly supply all your needs if *you give him first place in your life*" (Matt. 6:31, 32 LB).

31.   Always keep open to more light. Light responded to and shared brings more light. But light unshared and rejected brings darkness.

32.   Blessed be humiliations. They are invitations to stay with our Lord the King, in his country house in the Valley of Humiliation, where he loves to spend much time surrounded by his friends (Bunyan).

33.   Be willing to learn through failures, even bitter ones. There may be many a slip in going down the hill, but for the going down I thank God still.

Chapter 9: Seventy Palm Trees (Exod. 15:27)

LAST LESSONS IN THE FRIENDS' EVANGELISTIC BAND

34.   When we are not sure if we are hearing God's guidance aright, always take the first step in trying to obey what we think he is telling us to do. Then he will either open the door and lead on step by step, or else he will completely block the way and so show us that we were not hearing aright.

35.   "Faith steps out onto the seeming void and finds the Rock beneath."

36.   Jesus said, "I am among you as he that serveth." Let this always be our own attitude too.

37. Sacrifice is the ecstasy of giving the best we have to the one we love the most.

Chapter 10: Food from Heaven in the Desert of Sibn (Exod. 16)

IRELAND'S EYE AND THE CALL TO PALESTINE

38. In thought and imagination practice becoming the people with whom we are in contact, especially those who need God's forgiving love and help. Learn to look through their eyes and to see things from their point of view and not just from our own.

39. Joyfully let God teach us how to love seemingly unlovely people. All unlovely things are really crying out piteously for help to become the beautiful things that God wants them to be.

40. Be blessedly afraid of allowing anything to allure us away from the path of God's will for us.

Chapter 11: Massab (Exod. 17:1–7)

ARRIVAL IN HAIFA AND PALESTINE

41. Everything begins in our thoughts and in the pictures that we imagine. Whatever we choose to think about and picture, we shall begin to express either in word or action.

42. Never picture ourselves doing anything, and never let self be in the center of anything we imagine and desire. The Lord Jesus must always be the central figure.

43. Be willing to see ourselves as others see us, and remember that anything we criticize in them is certainly to be found in ourselves too, though perhaps in another form, or we would not notice it in them. Then let God show us a picture of what he wants us to become—*just like Jesus*.

Chapter 12: The Amalekites (Exod. 17:8–13)

TIMES OF TERRORISM AND TESTINGS

44.   When we feel that we cannot forgive and forget what others do to us and to our loved ones, let us take the whole matter to the cross of Jesus and ask him to forgive those who are doing the wrong things and our own wrong unforgiving reactions to them. Then leave the whole matter at the cross and promise the Lord that we will never mention it again to anyone else or to ourselves in thought, even if the wrongs continue to be done day after day. When we stop talking to ourselves in thought and to others about it, then the wrong things done to us and our own wrong reactions will not be able to harm us. The bitter feelings will gradually fade away, and some lovely blessing will begin springing up instead. We shall have power to help others, including the wrongdoers, in a way never before possible.

45.   Never say or do anything that we know the Lord Jesus himself would not say or do if we could see him present in the circumstances in which we find ourselves. Claim his grace to act and react just as he would.

46.   When Jesus was filled with compassion he was able to heal the sick: liberate slaves to sin and work mighty miracles. Let us beg him to teach us to be compassionate toward all wrongdoers just as he was. Let us see them as sin-sick souls expressing agonizing symptoms and disease and begging for help and healing, under the guise of causing suffering to others.

Chapter 13: Jehovah Nissi, the Lord Our Banner
(Exod. 17:15, 16)

VISITING EVERY PLACE WITH BIBLES AND NEW TESTAMENTS

47.   Learn to lift up a faithful, loving banner of witness to the saving power of Christ wherever we are led to follow him among

those who know nothing about him and need to hear the good news.

48.   The inspired Scriptures are like heavenly dynamite, and they are to be placed wherever the Holy Spirit gives us the opportunity to do so. Then believe and claim that the time will come when he will light the fuse, and an explosion of glorious, life-bringing revival will take place.

Chapter 14: Jethro, the Priest of Midian (Exod. 18:1–10)

LIGHT RECEIVED THROUGH A MOSLEM WOMAN AND AN ORTHODOX JEW

49.   The Savior of all wins a one hundred percent victory and the devil gets none. God has pledged himself to save every single soul, and not one of them will be lost. We do experience self-made hells, but none of them are endless.

50.   In Hebrew the term *endless* can be only applied to God himself, and to no one and nothing else. He alone is the eternal endlessly existing being. In Hebrew and Greek, the word *everlasting* does not mean "endless" but "as long as time lasts." Time is not endless; it is only an experience of our fallen, temporary world.

51.   Not only will all fallen souls be restored to our lost God-consciousness and joyful union with God's will, but we will also be able to love and adore him to a greater degree than would be possible if we had not fallen. We could never have realized the height and depth and breadth and length of God's forgiving love or been able to know him as he really is, for there would have been no opportunity to see the full, glorious revelation of his nature and character. True indeed are the Savior's words, "He that is forgiven much, loveth much."

52.   All the hells are experienced here on earth. We see them all around us in the conditions experienced by those in the Third World of homeless refugees and terrorist activities, persecutions

and cruelties of all kinds, also in the haunts of drug addicts, alcoholics, and slaves of vice. They are everywhere, and not in some mythical imaginary lake of fire and brimstone. That is a symbolic description of all the burning, purging torments experienced by those here on earth who are the slaves of sin.

53. Every hell is a purging, purifying experience which completely burns away all further desire to continue as slaves to our own self-will. It is the purging pains of hell that awaken passionate desire to recover our lost God-consciousness.

54. All who die unsaved return to earth again and experience a self-made hell. But those who meet the Lord and Savior Jesus Christ in an earth lifetime and respond to him are born again and begin to experience eternal life, and, like the angels, "they will die no more." That is, they will not need to return to yet another lifetime here on earth. All the Old Testament saints believed this and confirmed it.

Chapter 15: The Workers Who Helped Moses (Exod. 18:14–21)

EVACUATION 1947

55. The heavenly spheres are full of music and blissful harmonies that pour forth consolation and tender sympathy to those who suffer and have no human helpers.

56. Whenever we feel a strong leading to pray about the special needs of others, we must be ready and on the watch to be shown if God wills to use us in helping to meet those needs.

57. It is always safe to put our hand in the hand of the loving Lord and with him to go up to all impossible-looking challenges, knowing that he will open up the way and lead into greater blessing than we have ever known.

58. How often we can say with hearts overflowing with joy, "This is the day I so much dreaded—and it hasn't happened!"

Even when a day full of seeming terror dawns before us, we can exultantly exclaim, "This is the day the Lord has made, we will be glad and rejoice in it!"

59.   Everything voluntarily laid down into death at the Lord's command will be raised again in some more glorious form.

Chapter 16: The Mountain Smoked (Exod. 19:1–20)

THE SIEGE OF JERUSALEM, 1948

60.   "I will say of the Lord, he is my refuge ... In him will I trust." Though the enemy drops a thousand shells or shoots a thousand bullets, no evil can befall us. "For he gives his angels charge over us to keep us in all our ways" (Ps. 91).

61.   "The name of the Lord is a strong tower. The righteous runneth into it and is safe" (Prov. 18:10).

Chapter 17: The Thick Darkness Where God Was
(Exod. 20:18–21)

THE WAILING WOMEN; THE LITTLE DOG

62.   If we abide in the Lord's presence snuggled close to him, the shining angels will know that we are a part of him, and they will take us wherever they go with him.

63.   Let us learn the lesson taught by the flocks of white pigeons, which every evening rose up from both sides of the divided city and mingled happily together in the sky in peaceful companionship, as though there was no war-wracked city below but only brotherhood and sisterhood and goodwill.

64.   "*Ouai! Ouai!* Alas! Alas! How often I would have gathered you as a hen gethers her chicks beneath her wings. But you would not come. Alas, alas, for the sorrow and desolation which

you are preparing for yourselves, and the *woes* you are bringing upon yourselves. But I, the Savior, will share them with you and bring you out of all the woeful desolations which you are creating for yourselves. Yes, I will bring you right back to the loving heart of our Father, and all your lamenting will cease and be turned into rapturous joy."

65.   "Write the things which you have heard and seen, and share them with others," so that they also may come to know the same blessed truth and heavenly lessons.

Chapter 18: On the Mount with God
(Exod. 23:20–25; 24:16–18)

MY FATHER'S DEATH AND THE FRIENDS AT ZURICH AIRPORT

66.   Enter the deep darkness where God is (Exod. 20:21), and build altars where God tells you to.

67.   Go through each day praising and thanking God for everything that happens—the seemingly unpleasant things as well as the good ones. For praising God is like using a holy magic wand which, when waved over disagreeable things, will change them into the opposite forms of goodness. Learn from the Lord how to become heavenly magicians.

Chapter 19: The Glory of the Lord on the Mountaintop
(Exod. 24:17, 18)

MOUNT OLYMPUS IN CYPRUS

68.   Learn the glorious secret of how to experience a transformed thought life and cleansed lips and speech habits. Study the heavenly language called Blessing, which means "speaking well of everything," expressing positives only and no negatives.

69.   Live practicing this glorious transformed thought life and "the Lord your God will take away sickness from the midst of you" (Exod. 23:25).

Chapter 20: "Building a Sanctuary for the Lord to Dwell In (Exod. 25:1, 2, 8)

LEARNING TO BE AN ARROW IN GOD'S QUIVER AND ENLISTING AN ARMY OF INTERCESSORS AROUND THE WORLD

70.   Every altar of surrender will produce a harvest of much fruit to enjoy with the loving Lord at some time in the future.

71.   If there is one person in the world you do not want to love, then you really know nothing about God's love (William Law). For God is love and he is immanent in every human soul.

72.   All human souls are living cells united together to form one body, of which the Lord Jesus is the head. Everything we do to each other we do to ourselves and also to our heavenly Father Creator; for the Lord Jesus himself spoke for God and said, "Inasmuch as you have done it unto one of the least of these my brethren, you have done it unto me."

Let us pray for a new attitude toward everyone, which will enable us to say in thought, "You are part of me and I am part of you. We shall experience the results of everything we do to each other. So I must love you as I love myself because you are really a part of me as I am of you."

73.   God feels, bears, and forgives the sins of the whole world. He allows his own loving consciousness to be nailed with us to the cross of suffering that fallen human beings make for ourselves. But all the time he is also rising up in consciousness from the cross with and in those who are being led to understand and to respond to his grace and love.

74.   All suffering is atoning, and it purges and heals. Not one drop of it is wasted. God uses it all in his ministry of purging and healing other sin-sick souls.

Chapter 21: A Mercy Seat of Pure Gold (Exod. 25:17, 22, 40)

OUTSIDE THE CAMP, AND THE CAMPS FARTHEST OUT

76.   The darkest hour is just before the dawn, and the greater the darkness, the brighter the dawn will be.

77.   Never be hurt when others reject or ostracize us. Remember that the only thing in us that can be hurt is pride, and the sooner that is dealt with, the better it will be in every way. So as Jesus bids us do, rejoice and praise God, even for real persecution, for it helps us to go "farther on and higher up" to still more heavenly places.

78.   Our bodies cooperate in helping us to understand which Kingdom of Heaven principles we need to develop to a still higher degree of perfection and which ones are definitely unheavenly. Every symptom of physical pain and disease manifested in our bodies is a challenge to go to the Savior's consulting room. There we can ask him to diagnose our spiritual need and to prescribe a heavenly attitude that we need to practice in order to recover our spiritual health. Then healing for the body will follow, unless we still need to experience it longer in order to be protected from some special temptation that we still are not spiritually developed enough to meet and overcome.

79.   There is a mercy seat of pure gold, where the Divine Doctor and Surgeon of sin-sick souls is ever willing to receive us and prescribe a course of blessed remedial treatment for spirit, soul, and body.

Chapter 22: The Cherubim on the Mercy Seat (Exod. 25:18–23)

SPECIAL LESSONS LEARNED WITH THE CAMPS FARTHEST OUT

80.   Be careful never to tell anyone, or ourselves, that we may do something that the Lord Jesus in his teaching in the Sermon on the Mount said should not be done.

81.   If you love enough, you can bear any amount of pain triumphantly and even rejoice in it.

82.   In the end, pain purges away all desire to continue sinning. It is a divine antiseptic of great value.

83.   Say in thought to everyone you meet, "You are one of my brothers or sisters. *Can I Help You?*" CIHU (Dr. Frank Laubach).

84.   Bodies are to be offered to God to be temples in which his Holy Spirit can dwell and which he can use for holy purposes.

85.   The Christ light of God's love shines around every human being, waiting for them to open themselves and invite him to enter and fill them with the life and love of God. (Tillie Baxter).

86.   Let no idle or useless words ever proceed out of our mouths; but let us always speak and behave as messengers of the Holy One. Let's sit like the cherubim upon the mercy seat, and use our lips to express God's love.

Chapter 23: Show Me Thy Glory (Exod. 33:11–19)

HOLY HARMLESSNESS

87.   The Creator is immanent in all living creatures, not just in human beings. He feels in the fish, birds, and animals just as he feels in us. All we do to them we do to him too. Everything that happens in the slaughterhouses around the world, and through our Twentieth-century factory farming processes, as well

as all that goes on in experimental vivisection laboratories, he feels as being done to him.

88.   Anything we would not wish to have done to us we must never do to any other living creature, for sometime we shall have to experience all that we willfully cause them and their Creator to feel.

89.   Let us become Garden of Eden people again, and nourish our bodies with plant food only, just as God ordained in Genesis 1:29. We are to eat fruits, plants, and all the grains or seeds that grow so abundantly all over the world. The birds and animals must do so too (Gen. 1:30).

90.   No living being or creature must prey upon others or kill and eat any flesh. All who do sentence themselves to have their own bodies killed and eaten by disease and death.

91.   Full restoration to God's original ideal for us is promised in Isaiah 11:6–8 (KJV): "The wolf also shall dwell with the lamb, and the leopard shall lie down with the kid . . . and a little child shall lead them. . . . The lion shall eat straw like the ox . . . They shall not hurt nor destroy in all my holy mountain, for the earth shall be full of the knowledge of the Lord as the waters cover the sea."

If we earnestly long and pray for that blessed time to come, then we must begin to live that way now and encourage others to do so too.

Chapter 24: A Merciful and Gracious God (Exod. 34:5–8)

THE SAMARITAN SACRIFICE ON MOUNT GERIZIM AND THE WHITE RABBIT

92.   "Thus saith the Lord, I delight not in the blood of bullocks and lambs and of goats. Your appointed feasts my soul hates, they are a trouble to Me . . . Your hands are full of blood" (Isa. 1:11–16).

93. *"Behold the lamb of God bearing the sins of the world."*

94. In the Garden of Eden, the living creatures were the loving friends and companions of humankind. We cannot kill, cook, and eat our friends.

Chapter 25: The Lord Will Do Marvels (Exod. 34:8–10)

SEEKING TO LIVE ACCORDING TO THE GARDEN OF EDEN WAY OF LIFE

95. Every altar of self-surrender leads to glorious enrichment. Every closed door means that the loving Lord will open another one and teach us how to serve him in some new and beautiful way, better than anything possible before.

96. Person-to-person witness is probably the most powerful and fruitful of all forms of witness.

97. Never try to force people to listen to us, but by holy, God-inspired example and daily conduct attract others to come and ask for counsel and help.

98. "He that receiveth a little child in my name receiveth me" was the blessed assurance of the Savior himself. So let us lovingly teach the little children to care about the living creatures, and also to talk to the Lord Jesus just as they would if they could see him. Then great and wonderful results will follow. Remember that the Savior says, "Suffer the little children to come unto me and forbid them not, for of such is the Kingdom of Heaven" (Mark 10:14).

Chapter 26: The Presence of God (Exod. 34:29, 30, 35)

CONFIRMING SIGNS THAT THE HARMLESS CANNOT BE HARMED

99. The Garden of Eden plant food for our bodies is a joy and satisfaction to the plants themselves. For the Creator has

implanted in them his own urge to give themselves and what they produce to be a blessing to others. So as soon as their seeds and fruits are ripe they long to give them away to the birds, animals, and human beings. If no one picks them or gathers them, they let them fall to the ground, for the urge is so strong to give them away and to replenish the earth with more. We give them what they long for most when we gather and accept all that they so freely offer to us.

100. *The harmless cannot be harmed*. Nothing in the universe has the power to injure anyone who never injures others. Either the desire to harm will be taken away from the would-be enemies, or else the power to do so, and they will become unable to carry out their evil intentions. The Lord Jesus demonstrated this fact again and again. Continually his enemies were seeking to kill him but could never do so, until at last he voluntarily laid aside his invulnerability and allowed them to take him and put him to death. So then he could demonstrate the loving forgiveness of God and rise again from the dead.

101. Remember that those who have more light than others and willfully do what they know is not God's highest and best will become more vulnerable than others to danger and harm than those with less light or none at all and who thus continually and ignorantly do what is not good.

In Luke 12:48 we read that those who are not aware that they are doing wrong will be punished only lightly. But much is required from those to whom much is given, for their responsibility is greater. So those who have much light will be severely punished if they do wrong; for though they know their duty they refuse to do it. (See Luke 12:47 LB.)

102. The Law of the Lord ordains that we punish ourselves when we do wrong, for we always gravitate to the results of what we do and we experience them. This law shows us that the only

way in which it can be said that God punishes sinners is that he permits them to punish themselves.

103.   Let us pray that we may abide so closely beside our Lord, that the glow of his presence will cause an aura of holy influence to surround us, which will help others to dread doing harm to any living creature.

Chapter 27: Holiness in the Lord
(Exod. 34:10–12; 35:4–29; 36:5)

RETURN TO TRAVEL

104.   Be very, very careful never to compromise in any way when seeking to obey God's will. For if we do so we shall soon be following evil ways.

105.   It is a great privilege to be invited to enter the Secret Service of the Lord and to abide hidden in the secret place of the Most High; for then we shall remain safely protected from the persecutions, revilings, and slanders that threaten those who use paid publicity methods in order to draw great multitudes of people to listen to the messages. A great number, perhaps the majority of listeners at publicized meetings, will not be ready and willing to respond to the Savior's message. Some will come seeking release from their pain and troubles or else out of curiosity. Many more will come in order to cause difficulties and to attack the ministry in some way.

106.   Never use worldly means in order to gain hearers, but draw individuals to listen by means of the personal example of a holy, God-centered life.

107.   Thankfully remember that we are lovingly warned how the apostle Peter learned to stop using publicity methods in order to gather great crowds to listen to the gospel message. Per-

secution broke out. He was arrested, beaten, and finally cast into prison under sentence of death (Acts 12:1–17). When he was miraculously delivered by an angel, he was led to retire into the Lord's Secret Service, and from Acts 12:17 we hear not a single word more about Peter nor anything that he did and taught.

108.   The desire to gather as many people as possible to listen to the good news, can all too easily awaken another desire in our hearts, namely to show off how the Lord loves to use us in his service, and how he makes us his favorite instruments in delivering others. The desire to outshine other faithful people will lead to the most afflicting of all forms of bondage.

109.   Let us rejoice that we can always learn through our mistakes and be able to warn others against making them too. Blessed be failures and their consequences, through which we learn what we were ignorant of before. As the psalmist said, "Before I was afflicted I went astray, but now have I kept thy word" (Psalm 119:67 KJV).

110.   By learning and practicing the blessed lessons God teaches us in the School of Earth Experience, our minds and bodies become holy sanctuaries in which the Holy Spirit can dwell, and which he can use to God's glory (Exod. 36:4).

Chapter 28: The Glory of the Lord Filled the Tabernacle (Exod. 40:33–38)

THE LAND OF GOD'S FULFILLED PROMISES

111.   By means of the Book of Memory, we can recall the priceless, enriching lessons and truths that God has taught us all through the years. Thus we can trace the seed-sowing causes from which rich harvests of fruitfulness and God-given blessings have sprung up, and the joyous experiences that blossom in the Land of his Fulfilled Promises.